IoTization

How to Transform Your Company and Win the
Internet of Things

SHU LIU

ISBN: 978-1-0806-4898-6

DEDICATION

To my wife, Gusui Zhang

CONTENTS

ACKNOWLEDGMENTS

I would like to thank all those who helped me complete this book.

To the entire review team from the American Society for Quality, for their tremendous effort in analyzing the strength and weakness of the manuscript and their valuable suggestions and recommendations.

To Janina Lawrence, who did a terrific job editing the manuscript. She went to great lengths to correct errors in spelling and grammar.

To all my friends and family members, for their encouragement and patience.

To my wife, Gusui Zhang, for her unconditional love and support. Without her this book is not even possible.

Finally, to all my readers, for their interest and feedback that give me a sense of purpose and inspire me to keep writing.

PREFACE

I have spent my entire career in semiconductor, chemical, and material industries, serving in various managerial capacities for R&D, quality, and engineering functions. Throughout those years as a seasoned professional specialized in process optimization and machine learning, I have led many programs and projects of technology upgrade. At the same time, I have seen many companies fall behind competitors because they couldn't keep up with the rapid technology advancement.

Business leaders and managers are reading headlines every day about the Internet of Things (IoT). They are told that they must get on the IoT train to stay on the top of competition. But how should they do it?

Contrary to what many people think, transforming your company to embrace the IoT, the endeavor I call IoTization, does not require you to learn and adopt many novel and fancy business theories and methodologies. The sound business practices such as Hoshin strategic planning (also called Hoshin Kanri) and conventional techniques for business improvement will help you get there, as illustrated below. This is what this book is about.

There are four parts to this book.

Part 1 discusses what the IoT is (chapter 1) and why you must embrace it (chapter 2).

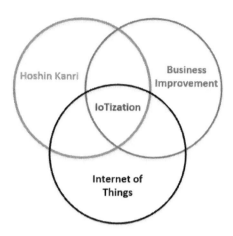

Part 2 discusses how to study where you are today from the IoT perspective—your current state. Chapter 3 explores understanding the voice of the customer (VOC) and how to collect VOC data from both IoT and non-IoT customers. Chapter 4 discusses how to comprehend your company's situation today—your current business models, business processes, your strengths, weaknesses, opportunities, and threats. It holds some real IoT applications in business model development and in process mapping. It also discusses, in depth, the use of business model canvas, the application of IoT business model patterns and business model pattern matrixes. Chapter 5 is about investigating your business environment by studying your competitors, benchmarking the IoT leaders, and analyzing social, technological, economic, environmental, and political factors in your business environment. It specifically discusses how to evaluate competitors' IoT business models and how they fit the patterns of IoT business models.

Part 3 is about figuring out where you want to be in the IoT world—your future state. Chapter 6 explains how to develop your vision and your business objectives. A large portion of chapter 6 is devoted to analyzing vision statements of famous IoT companies (Apple, Amazon, and Google) and using them as examples in discussing how to develop an organization's vision. Chapter 7 shows you how to develop your business strategies and new business models based on your business strategies. It leads readers into an exercise of laying out

Google's business strategies based on its vision statement and information from the company's website. When discussing the process of developing IoT business models, the chapter presents opportunities for each pattern of IoT business models. Chapter 8 demonstrates the management process for developing IoT products. It presents a roadmap for IoT product development which has been adapted by a handful of IoT companies. Chapter 9 discusses, function by function, how to develop an IoT organization.

Part 4 is a large tool box. Chapter 10 explores how to analyze VOC data, using tools such as the affinity diagram, the Kano model, quality function deployment, and conjoint analysis. It takes the case of an IoT mailing company Pitney Bowes to show how to use VOC analysis tools for Pitney's business. Chapter 11 and chapter 12 cover tools for product development. Chapter 11 shows, with some real IoT examples, how to use tools for IoT product development such as the Pugh matrix, failure mode and effects analysis (FMEA), design scorecards, and the theory of inventive problem solving (TRIZ). Chapter 12 discusses two design techniques—the axiomatic design and the Taguchi robust parameter design, and how to use them on IoT applications.

The journey to IoTization is challenging and exciting. I hope this book will help you get there. Enjoy.

PART ONE

WHAT AND WHY?

I can't understand why people are frightened of new ideas. I'm frightened of the old ones.

– John Cage

CHAPTER ONE

WHAT IS THE IOT?

There are a lot of talks these days about the Internet of Things and about its impact on every aspect of our lives. But what is the Internet of Things? How does it work?

DEFINITION

The Internet of Things, known as the IoT, is a global infrastructure for the information society, enabling advanced services by interconnecting (physical and virtual) things based on existing and evolving interoperable information and communication technologies, as defined by Telecommunication Standardization Sector of International Telecommunication Union.[1] It is a system in which physical things connect with each other and exchange virtual things in a network. The physical things are objects of the physical world, consisting of machines such as devices, vehicles, home appliances, and embedded electronics such as sensors, CPU architectures, operating systems, and electronic packaging.

The virtual things are data of the information world. The current Internet collects data generated by people when they search, purchase, and communicate online. It is the Internet of People. The next generation of the Internet collects data from physical things—

things in the physical world that can be sensed, actuated, and connected while the virtual things in the information world can be stored, processed, and accessed.[1]

The IoT allows communication to occur with anything, at any time, and in any place. Anything communication means communication occurring between computers, between people without using computers, between people and things, and between things directly. Anytime communication refers to communication taking place at night or during the daytime. Any place communication means that communication occurs when people are either outdoors or indoors, or when they are either away from the computer or with the computer.

REFERENCE MODEL

There are four layers in the IOT reference model proposed by the Telecommunication Standardization Sector of International Telecommunication Union: device layer, network layer, service support and application support layer, and application layer. Associated with the four layers are management and security capabilities, as shown in Figure 1.0.[1]

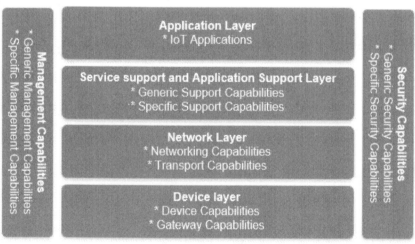

Fig. 1.0: IoT Reference Model

DEVICE LAYER

There are two kinds of capabilities in the device layer: device capabilities and gateway capabilities. Device capabilities directly or indirectly gather and upload data to the communication network and receive data from the network. Devices can also construct networks in an ad-hoc manner to enhance scalability and deployment speed.[1] Gateway capabilities support devices to connect to networks with different protocols. Major physical components in the device layer are imbedded sensors, central processing units (CPUs), software, and electronic packaging.[2]

SENSORS

A sensor is a device or a module that detects changes in a machine and sends information to other electronics. Types of sensors are numerous, such as: acceleration/vibration, acoustic/ultrasonic, chemical/gas, electric/magnetic flow, force/load/torque/strain, humidity/moisture, leak/level, optical, motion/velocity/displacement, position/presence/ proximity, pressure, and temperature.[3] Sensors can be embedded within the product during the design or in a retrofired product.[4]

CENTRUAL PROCESSING UNITS (CPUs)

A CPU is an electronic circuitry that performs basic algorithm and input/output operations specified by a computer program. Typically, there are two components in a CPU, the arithmetic logic unit (ALU) and the control unit (CU). An ALU performs arithmetic and logical operations while a CU decodes and executes instructions from memory. Basic CPUs such as Arduino have limited access to memory storage and consume limited power. Advanced RISC Machines (ARM) and Intel Atom are two examples of advanced CPUs.[2]

SOFTWARE

Software enables the physical things to interface with each other. When you select a software for the IoT applications, consider the requirements for the memory footprints, integrated development environment (IDE), and real-time operating systems (RTOSs).[2] Memory footprint indicates the amount of a program's memory. An IDE is a software application that facilitates computer programs' software development. A RTOS is an operating system serving real-time data processing without buffer delay.

ELECTRONIC PACKAGING

Electronic packaging refers to the features built into electronic products that protect the products from mechanical damage, cooling, radio frequency noise emission, and electronic discharge. System-on-a-chip (SoC) and system-in-package (SiP) are two examples of electronic packaging technologies.[2]

NETWORK LAYER

The network layer has two capabilities: the networking capabilities and the transport capabilities.

NETWORKING CAPABILITIES

The networking capabilities transfer network packets from a source to a destination host. They identify addresses of the neighboring nodes in the network, combine outputs with correct network address information, select routes and quality of service, and forward incoming messages for local host domains to the transport layer. The Internet Protocol (IP) part of TCP/IP (both IP Version 4 and IP Version 6) and NetWare IPX/SPX are existing protocols in the network layer.

TRANSPORT CAPABILITIES

The transport capabilities provide connectivity to transport and manage IoT service and application specific information. They ensure reliable arrival of messages, provide error checking mechanisms, and control data flow for both "connection-mode" transmissions and "connectionless-mode" transmissions in a packet form.

SERVICE SUPPORT AND APPLICATION SUPPORT LAYER

This layer has capabilities of supporting different IoT applications such as data processing and data storage.

A large amount of data coming from the network layer must be collected and stored. In the service support and application layer, data is collected and stored using a variety of technologies, including structured query language (SQL) in a rational database management system (RDBMS), NoSQL, time series database (TSDB), heterogeneous database system (HDB), and cloud computing.[2]

STRUCTURED QUERY LANGUAGE IN A RATIONAL DATABASE MANAGEMENT SYSTEM

SQL is a domain-specific programing language that consists of many sublanguages. SQL is responsible for data query, data manipulation, data definition, and data access control. Unlike the older language versions, SQL can access many records with one single command, and it does not need to specify the ways to reach a record. SQL is designed for managing data in relational database management system (RDBMS), a database management system based on the relational model.[5]

NoSQL A NoSQL database is used for storing and retrieving data using different models from the tabular relations used in relational databases. The major NoSQL database models include key-value store, column-oriented store, document-oriented store, and graph database. NoSQL is a better choice than SQL when data requirements are unrelated or indeterminate, or project objectives are not complicated, or speed and scalability is imperative.[2]

TIME SERIES DATABASE

A time series is a series of data points taken at successive time intervals. The traditional relational databases are not modeled correctly for time series and they do not operate well in queries and in database transactions between different time zones. Time series databases (TSDBs) impose models for time series. With TSDBs, users can create, enumerate, update, and remove various time series and organize them hierarchically or horizontally with other metadata bases; eXtremeDB, Graphite, InflusDB, Informix time series, Kx kdb+, Riak-TS, and RRDtool are some examples of TSDBs. HETEROGENEOUS DATABASE If users want a single, unified query interface for data from heterogeneous, disparate database management systems, heterogeneous databases (HDBs) is the best choice. Hadoop and Splunk are two examples of HDBs. Hadoop stores and processes large volumes of data from heterogeneous database systems. The basic structure of Hadoop consists of a distributed file system called HDFS and a data processing model called MapReduce. Splunk provides system administrators with a great degree of flexibility in analyzing data coming from a system's hardware or software.[2]

CLOUD COMPUTING

Cloud computing provides users with the share pools of configurable system resources and higher-level services over the Internet. It achieves coherence and economies of scales with minimal management effort through multiple cloud components that communicate with each other over a loose coupling mechanism. The major service models of cloud computing include infrastructure as a service (IaaS), platform as a service (PaaS), software as a service (SaaS), mobile "backed" as a service (MBaaS), and serverless computing. The deployment models of cloud computing can be private, public, or hybrid.[6]

APPICATION LAYER

The application layer provides an initial set of communication protocols and interface methods to ensure the effective communication between application programs.

Many statistical techniques are applied to analyze the rich data in the application layer. Among them, regression analysis, time series analysis, and multivariate analysis are the frequently used tools.

REGRESSION ANALYSIS

Regression analysis is the major analytical tool in data analytics.[7] Regression analysis builds a regression model that describes the relationship between predictors and response variables. The model is then used to predict future outcomes. Least square regression, orthogonal regression, and partial least square regression are used for continuous data. Logistic regressions are used for binary, ordinal, and nominal data while Poisson regression is for analyzing count data.

TIME SERIES ANALYSIS

For the historical time series data, techniques in time series analysis such as trend analysis, decomposition, autocorrelation, and autoregressive integrated moving average (ARIMA) are used to create an approximating function for future forecasting. Usually, time series data sets have a lot of noise that need to be taken out in order to capture important patterns in the data. This type of data treatment is called data smoothing that is performed using several smoothing methods such as moving average, exponential smoothing, and winter's method.[8]

MULTIVARIATE ANALYSIS

Multivariate analysis is applied to analyze the covariance structure of data, to assign observations to groups, and to explore relationships between categorical data. Principle component analysis and factor analysis are two major tools for data structure analysis. Cluster analysis and discriminant analysis are used for data grouping, and correspondent analysis is for simple or multiple classifications.[9]

MANAGEMENT CAPABILITIES

The IoT's management capabilities manage fault, configuration, accounting, performance and security. They include device management, local network management, and traffic and congestion management.

SECURITY CAPABILITIES

The IoT's security capabilities cover the following areas:

1. Data confidentiality and integrity protection, privacy protection, security audit, and antivirus at the application layer

2. Data confidentiality and signaling integrity protection at the network layer

3. Device integrity validation, access control, data confidentiality,

and integrity protection at the device layer

The IoT enables individuals and companies to speed up automation and integration within a system. It brings major changes in producing and

delivering products, goods, and services, creating significant social, economic and political impact. Even in its infant stage, the IoT has already found a wide range of applications. The evolution of the IoT technologies will find unlimited applications in nearly all the fields, which will be discussed in more detail in the next chapter.

CHAPTER TWO

WHY THE IOT?

The current Internet collects data from people—the data generated by people when they do online searches, purchases, and communication. So we call it the Internet of People (IoP). The next generation of Internet, the Internet of Things (IoT), collects data from things—the data generated by devices and machines used by people. The IoT is more powerful than the IoP because there will be many more things than people, and things can generate much more data than people do. John Chambers, the former CEO of Cisco, estimated that there will be 500 billion things connected by 2024, about hundred times more than the number of people on the planet.1 Furthermore, when everything is equipped with sensors, and each of those sensors constantly generates data, the amount of data is much more than the data generated by people on the Internet.

THE IOT EVOLUTION

Since the IoT started to spread in the early 2000s, two major steps have laid a foundation for future development.

The first step was taken by supply chain helpers who used radio frequency identification (RFID) tags to facilitate routing, inventorying, and loss prevention to meet the demand for expedited logistics. The second step started with vertical market applications including surveillance, security, healthcare, transport, food safety, and document management. As a result, cost is significantly reduced, and that leads to a broader scope for improvement and implementation of the IoT technologies. We are now in the middle of the third step and the early stage of the fourth step. The third step involves ubiquitously positioning people and everyday objects accomplished by positioning systems, which is more sophisticated than the phase of RFID. On the fourth step, physical world webs will be developed that will use teleoperation and telepresence GPS to monitor and control distant objects. The new IoT technologies will be enabled by miniaturization, power-efficient electronics, and available spectrum. The technology roadmap of the IoT is show in Figure 2.0.[2]

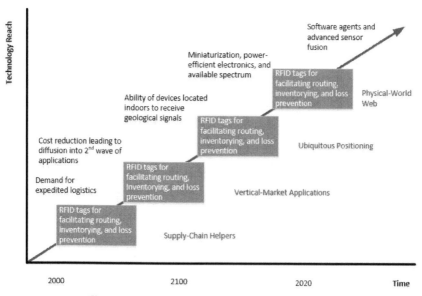

Fig. 2.0: Technology Roadmap of the IoT

Security remains as the largest challenge throughout the IoT evolution, and it is the greatest roadblock for the IoT adoption. The most vulnerable area is infrastructure IoT, as successful attacks in communication, transportation, and power will cause disastrous consequences. Therefore, all companies must manage cybersecurity seriously, and governments must be involved in it through registration and regulation.[2]

WHY THE IOT?

The IoT is unleashing data that was previously inaccessible. It will connect everyone and everything in a seamless network which will dramatically affect the lives of everybody on the planet. The sky of the IoT is unlimited—its applications will be in nearly every aspect of human society, both on consumers and on enterprise.

The consumer IoT provides consumers with new experiences and interface, in connected cars, smart homes and devices, entertainment, wearable technology, quantified self, connected health—the list will go on and on. The enterprise IoT is used in media, infrastructure management, manufacturing, agriculture, energy management, environmental monitoring, building and home automation, metropolitan scale deployments, healthcare, and transportation. It is estimated that by 2019, nearly 40 percent or 9.1 billion devices used in business and corporate settings will be IoT devices. By 2020, 20 percent of computers will learn not only to process, but also work and manage things and humans.[3]

The IoT is a game changer. With rapid changes in technology and in the marketplace, every company has only one choice: you either adapt or you will die. Early IoT adapters will have distinctive advantages over latecomers. These companies will have a continuous flow of data from their production lines and from their customers. The rich data flow will enable them to serve their customers with asset management, predictive maintenance, and other on-time services. The IoT companies can continuously improve their products, quickly building differentiating value. This practice will help the IoT companies to refine their organizational structures and it will change their business models from making a single sale to receiving a recurrent, predictable flow of money.[4]

Since the number of ecosystems in each market is limited, entering the IoT market early will help companies to develop an ecosystem before their competitors do. Within each ecosystem, the number of players is also limited. The early arrivers will have a competitive advantage to fill in the limited spots.

Early IoT adapters will accumulate their knowledge and develop their unique technologies, and their patents are formidable entry barriers for latecomers. They will attract the IoT talents and keep them before their competitors get in the market.[5]

EXAMPLES OF IOT APPLICATIONS

Although still in its infant stage, the IoT has already flexed its muscles, creating enormous values for early IoT adaptors. In his book, Precision, Principles, Practices and Solutions for the Internet of Things, Timothy Chou describes a series of cases of IoT applications in the manufacturing and services industries.[6]

THE IOT MAILING

Pitney Bowes, a provider of postage, mailing, shipping products and solutions, applies the IoT solution to create business value for its large-scale printing and mailing business. The company embedded hundreds of sensors on its inserters in the printing and mailing equipment that the company sells to its customers. The sensors send process data to local computers which are connected to the Internet through a Cisco 819 Integrated Service Router. Data then is transferred through the transport layer security (TLS) connection and then collected by GE's Predix platform. GE's analytics services perform data analysis through configuration, abstraction, and extensible modules. Through continuously monitoring inserters and issuing pre-failure alert, the IoT solution has significantly improved service quality and reduced service cost. Once an alarm appears that indicates a potential failure on an equipment at a customer site, service technicians will arrive there with the correct parts. With a large database that continuously receives data from customers, Pitney Bowes is developing benchmarks to help customers improve their productivity.

THE IOT TRAINS

New York Air Brake (NYAB) is a leading manufacturer for railroad braking systems, training simulators, and train control systems. NYAB has deployed its first IoT application LEADER that is integrated with the electronics on locomotives to generate real-time information. Three platforms are deployed to collect the sensor data and send data to a software. The communication management units (CMUs) on the locomotives manage and optimize the data traffic routes, sending data to NYAB's cloud via Wi-Fi, cellular, or satellite. NYAB's cloud decompresses data and stores it in a time-series database. The time-series data can be retrieved at any time for any particular trip. LEADER uses machine learning (ML) technology to compare the actual train operation with the computer-generated plan and to monitor the health of the locomotive. Data is also used to predict and prescribe the brake shoe wear. The LEADER implementation has saved 10.8 million gallons of diesel fuel and has eliminated 109,500 metric tons of greenhouse gas emissions. By reducing coupler fatigue, wheel wear, and brake-shoe wear, LEADER has reduced maintenance cost, and has significantly increased throughput of transportation operation.

THE IOT MINING

Joy Global, a leading producer of mining systems, equipment, parts, and services, is an earlier adapter of the IoT in the mining industry. The shearer on its Longwall mining machine cuts coal from a mine wall. The consolidated controller unit (CCU) installed on the machine monitors and controls the movement of the shearing arms and the powered roof support. Data from CCU is sent to a time-series database in the data center on the surface. Data is then analyzed to develop a predictive model. Joy Global uses the models for predictive maintenance on oil, gearbox or bearing, water jacket, and roof support. Joy Global's IoT solution that consists of the smart, connected machines, the advanced analytics, and the predictive maintenance services creates value for their customers. With the IoT implementation, the company has changed its business model from selling the equipment up-front to charging maintenance services based on a dollar-per-ton-mined metric that generates continuous revenues.

THE IOT GENE SEQUENCERS

Illumina, a market leader in gene sequencers, has developed its IoT product, MiniSeg, a DNA sequencing system which has more than forty embedded sensors. Data from the sensors is stored in a computer that runs a real-time operating system from Express Logic.

The computer is connected to the Illumina cloud where Illumina software schedules ETL (extraction, transformation, and loading) tasks for the machine data. Separate tools are used to store and analyze genomic data. The machine data is analyzed using a variety of software to calculate machine performance such as instrument utilization, uptime and downtime metrics, and to discern customer behavior, software adoption, and system-fault frequencies. Once data analytics has detected the early signs of machine performance problems, the company immediately sends technicians to the customer site to conduct preventive maintenance. The IoT solution has increased Illumina's service quality with reduced service cost.

THE IOT AGRICULTURE

AGCO Corporation is a large producer of agricultural equipment. It has implemented its IOT solutions on some of its product lines. For example, AGCO's Gleaner brand combine is equipped with many sensors and data from all machines that go through AGCO's Connectivity Module (ACM) and is transmitted to a server through a cellular network or satellite. Machine data, with customers' agreement, is stored in AGCO's SQL database running on Microsoft Azure's cloud service. Agronomic data is stored in a set of APIs that can be pulled by Farm Works Farm Managements Information System. Data analytics allows AGCO's dealers to provide farmers with high-quality and low-cost maintenance service. For example, once the machine data analytics indicates a machine that requires attention, the dealer notifies the farmer to stop the machine and recommends operations to avoid machine breakdown, or the dealer can send a service technician to replace the problematic parts. AGCO's IoT solution has changed dealers' business models from selling machines up front to charging machine as a service for large customers. In the new business model, farmers pay for machine hours and dealers provide predictive maintenance service that guarantees a minimum of 87 percent machine uptime.

THE IOT BUILDINGS

McKenny's Inc. is a mechanical contractor for building services including heating, ventilating, and air conditioning (HVAC), plumbing, maintenance, and building automation and control systems. It implemented a new energy management system at Eglin Air Force Base (Eglin). In Eglin's more than one hundred buildings, there are 20,000 sensors embedded in thousands of devices such as chillers, electric meters, thermostat, and variable air volume (VAV) controllers. Many of these devices are connected to Tridium Niagara Framework that provides Internet connection while maintaining the determinism and integrity required for real-time control. The network hardware is monitored by an InterMapper server. Data is stored in a SQL server and is sent to the Splunk indexer which performs search, reporting, and statistical analysis. The data analysis helps the Eglin base determine which HVAC systems can be shut off during high-cost periods. Data is also used on setting the structure-performance baselines and visualizing utility allocation. The IoT solution has saved the base 181 billion BTUs of electricity and natural gas, valued at $3.4 million. It has also reduced maintenance cost through predictive maintenance.

THE IOT CONSTRUCTION

Construction equipment rental companies rent thousands of units of construction equipment to their customers. Many of them are digitizing their businesses quickly. These IOT early adapters equip heavy equipment with fleet management devices such as Calamp LMU-5000, an on-board alert engine programmable event generator (PEG). PEG continuously monitors environmental conditions and supports predefined rules related to time, date, location, geo zone, and input. LMU-5000 provides connectivity through 3G Tri-band, packet radio, Wi-Fi and Iridium, or multiband highspeed packet access (HSPA). Data is saved in rental companies SQL databases, and from there, data can be pulled into enterprise resource planning (ERP) applications. Data can be sent from ERP to a data warehouse such as Teradata for reporting and analytics. The IoT solutions help rental companies reduce the service cost, improve product and service quality, lower consumable cost, and improve customers' health and safety. This is because the IOT early adapters are able to:

1. Identify what category and brand of units to purchase, and when and where to purchase them.

2. Estimate which brand is more cost-effective over the life of the

equipment.

3. Estimate safety stock.

4. Perform predictive maintenance that could easily save $100 million annually on a $1 billion spend.

5. Monitor equipment utilization along with alerts on rental contracts past due.

6. Recommend customers the right equipment to rent at different phases of their construction projects.

THE IOT HEALTHCARE

UC Irvine Medical Center has implemented its IOT solution to frequently monitor the heart rate, respiratory rates, and temperature of the patients who wear a SensiumVital patch. SensiumVital monitors the vital signs of patients and wirelessly sends data to clinicians via the hospital's IT network through a ZigBee-like protocol. Data is collected in an open-source software framework, the Hortonworks Hadoop, and in an electronic medical record (EMR) application. When the vital signs of a patient have crossed certain risk thresholds, the patient will be attended to immediately. Using the data collected, UC Irvine has built a predictive model that can identify which patients need resuscitation or other immediate medical attention, within ninety seconds of the event. The predictive medical intervention could, for example, reduce the death rate of premature, low-birth-rate babies. Without proper medical attention, 20 percent of them will develop an infection and 18 percent will die.

THE IOT OIL AND GAS

Modern deep-water oil and gas platforms are loaded with a variety of equipment such as pumps, compressors, and separators. These machines are equipped with many sensors, ranging anywhere from 20,000 to 40,000 in total on a platform. These sensors generate a variety of data such as time-series data, alarm data, event data, and maintenance and inspection data. These sensors are connected to a programmable logic controller (PLC) on the platform which is connected to a network by fiber optic cables. Data is collected both in supervisory control and data acquisition (SCADA) buffers and in the historian software databases. Over the last ten years, a number of predictive models have been developed that can predict equipment failure and send out early warning signs to platforms. In November 2013, for example, GE's IoT technology, SmartSignal detected abnormal pressure increases on a centrifugal compressor on a North Sea oil rig. After receiving the warning sign, technicians on the platform found that a malfunctioning seal-gas-control valve caused the high pressure and they repaired the valve immediately. Without the immediate intervention, the uncontrolled pressure could damage the 1200 HP compressor, shut down the production, contaminate environment, and even cause human injuries.

THE IOT POWER

Duck Energy is one of the largest electricity providers in the southeastern United States. Its phasor measurement unit (PMU) is a device that measures the electrical waves on electricity grids for synchronization. Duck Energy equips PMU with a GPS receiver to determine the location and time of power flow so that the power flow between the locations can be measured by comparing the phasor angles between locations. The data from PMUs is sent to a phasor data collator (PDC) through TCP/IP and is stored in SAS Enterprise Miner for analysis. Execution is managed through SAS' event stream processing (ESP). The decision tree statistic tool is used for event detection, identification, and qualification. An event is detected when there is a deviation from normal time-series patterns. The type of the detected event is then identified by matching its characteristics with those of the historical events of time-series clusters. Duck energy has developed special techniques to determine the magnitude of consequences of each type of events. Duck Energy uses its IoT solution to predict and prevent power disruption, providing tremendous value to the society. In the United States, the average hours of power disruption per consumer is nine hours which results in an estimated economical loss of at least $150 billion annually.

THE IOT FARMING

August Farms in the Cotswold area of England owns a seed drill, a solid fertilizer broadcast spreader, a liquid sprayer, and a combine. Its owner, Nick August, regularly uploads data of soil, yield, and aerial imagery into a farm management software to create prescription maps, and then uploads the maps into Topcon X30—a console with multiview interface on the seed drill for automatic control of the machine.

The solid fertilizer broadcast spreader also has a Topcon X30 that is connected with a LH Agro 5000 monitor and is integrated with GPS for automatic control of spreading rate.

The liquid sprayer also uses the Topcon X30 that controls sections, spray pump settings, and nozzle selection. It sends data of the spraying rate and machine settings to a USB thumb drive.

The combine harvester is equipped with AgCommand that controls the machine and sends data to the machine dealer. The combine also has a Topcon auto guidance embedded with agronomic satellite-based sensors to help operators maximize the machine capacity and reduce fatigue.

All data from machines is collected by a computer in Nick's office. Nick analyzes the yield maps, aerial images, and agronomic sensor scan to monitor crop development and to make decisions. With the IoT solution, Nick can predict potential output from each zone of the fields so he can treat each zone accordingly. The IoT solution also helps Nick reduce consumable cost.

THE IOT WATER

Bethel Farms grows turf and citrus near Arcadia, Florida. In 2009, the farm installed the McCrometer system that consists of water-flow meters, weather stations, and soil moisture meters. The sensors are connected wirelessly through an ultra-high frequency (UHF) radio or a general packet radio service (GPRS) cellular option to remote terminal units (RTUs) or to a collection management center based on HyerSQL. Data is used to identify malfunctioning irrigation systems and to create mathematical models for both ground water and surface water. The historical time-series data on soil moisture is used for forecasting future soil moisture readings. Combined with some infrastructure changes, Bethel Farms' IoT solution has reduced groundwater withdraws by 35 percent. The IoT solution can also predict plant disease outbreak by measuring and analyzing data from the disease triangle—the host, the disease, and the environment. That alone has avoided the net loss of $200 per acre over a 158-acre field in a large disease breakout.

THE IOT COOLING TOWER

Cooling tower, a mutual technology widely used in various industries and communities, has several drawbacks. First, it consumes large amounts of water. A single, middle-size cooling tower can consume millions of gallons of water annually. Second, harmful bacteria breed quickly in the warm water. These bacteria could lead to a Legionnaires' disease that occurs 8,000 to 18,000 per year in the United States. Third, untreated water can form calcium deposits that can clog pipes. The conventional way to kill the bacteria and to prevent deposits clogging is treating water with toxic chemicals—a process that consumes a large amount of water and pollutes environment.

Griswold Water Systems (GWS) has developed a new technology based on electric fields for water treatment. The electric fields generated by the GWS equipment injures bacteria and precipitates calcium in the water which is then removed by filtration. The equipment has a Netduino processor and some sensors that monitor cooling tower operating conditions, water flow, and water conductivity. Via a modem on the cooling tower and a 3G wireless connection, data is sent to Autodesk's IoT platform called Fusion Connect. Fusion Connect runs on an Amazon's cloud service and data is stored in a SQL Postgres and a NoSQL Cassandra databases infrastructure. On the Fusion Connect platform, operators can watch the cooling tower operation conditions. Once they receive an alert on a specific tower unit, they will repair the unit immediately. The IoT solution has reduced the operation cost through predictive maintenance and has eliminated the need for chemicals, resulting in reduction of water consumption up to 28 percent, valued at $25,000 per year per tower.

THE IOT RACE CAR

Sam Schmidt, a race car driver, was paralyzed from the neck down in a terrible car crash in January 2000. In order for Sam to drive again, an engineering group at Arrow Electronics built a semi-autonomous motorcar called the SAM Car. The car is equipped with a SAM computer that provides the gateway between cameras, sensors, the actuator control system, and the GPS unit. Here is how the system works: For steering, there are eight reflective infrared sensors fitted in the driver's sunglasses and four infrared cameras facing the driver. To steer, the driver just turns his head to the desired direction, the cameras and sensors track the head movement and send data into a single camera PC which connects to the SAM computer that controls the steering wheel.

For acceleration, the driver puffs breaths of air into a mouthpiece equipped with an NXP pressure sensor that sends a signal to a rotary actuator attached to the gas pedal. The gas pedal is depressed based on the amount of air pressure created by the driver.

For breaking, the driver sips on the same mouthpiece to create negative pressure. The breaking pedal is depressed based on the amount of the negative pressure created by the driver.

The Paravan drive system handles the actual control of the car. Its microprocessors transmit signals to braking, accelerating, and steering units. The SAM computer processes the data from sensors and cameras and sends messages to the Paravan system. The SAM computer is connected to the Arrow Connect Cloud through the onboard GPS unit over a 4G LTE modem. The Arrow Connect Cloud stores data from the SAM computer in its database. Data is used to visualize and analyze the interaction between the driver and the car. Driving the IoT race car in January 2016, Sam completed the Broadmoor Pikes Peak International Hill Climb in Colorado, reaching 80 miles per hour on some straightaways.

PART TWO

CURRENT STATE

If you know the enemy and know yourself, you need not fear the result of a hundred battles.

— Sun Tzu

CHAPTER THREE

WHAT IS THE CUSTOMER ASKING FOR?

From part 1 of this book, you have gained a lot of knowledge about the IoT and about why you must IoTize your company. But how are you going to do it? This is where strategic planning comes to play.

HOSHIN KANRI

Strategic planning is a business process for strategy development and implementation. Hoshin Kanri is a process for strategic planning.[1] The Hoshin Kanri process has four phases (Figure 3.0): determine the current state, develop the desired future state, develop strategies, and implement the strategies.

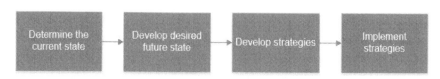

Fig. 3.0: Hoshin Kanri Process for Strategic Planning

DETERMINE THE CURRENT STATE

At this step, you collect data to understand what your customer wants and needs—the voice of the customer (VOC), how your company is doing today, how your competitors are doing, and what is your business environment.

DEVELOP DESIRED FUTURE STATE

After you have a good grasp on your current state, visualize your future state by creating your vision statement and your strategic objectives.

DEVELOP STRATEGIES At this step, decide on actions that you will take to achieve your business objectives. Your strategies should include actions to be taken at every level of your organization. These actions are usually a set of projects which are aligned with your business objectives.

IMPLEMENT STRATEGIES

With all the projects identified, use conventional project management tools to manage and execute your projects. Ensure these projects have sufficient resources to achieve their targets on time.

In part 2 of this book, we will discuss how to determine your current state from the IoT perspective. This chapter is about investigating the VOC from both industrial customers and IoT consumers. The next chapter (chapter 4) will discuss how to study your company's performance in the market segments that you are serving. Chapter 5 will discuss how to study your competitors' performance and your business environment.

Your IoTization journey starts with clearly understanding the VOC. Investigating the VOC for industrial customers is like that for IoT consumers, but there are some differences between the two. Let's discuss them separately.

VOC FROM INDUSTRIAL CUSTOMERS

There are several methods to use for collecting industrial VOC data, including customer interviews, focus groups, and surveys.

CUSTOMER INTERVIEW

Customer interviews are an effective market research technique that helps you maintain your market focus. Follow the well-defined, seven-step procedure to ensure the success of your customer interviews:

Step 1: Set objectives.

Step 2: Select customers to interview.

Step 3: Compose the interview team.

Step 4: Develop the discussion guide.

Step 5: Conduct the interviews.

Step 6: Debrief after each interview.

Step 7: Analyze interview data.[2]

Step 1: Set Objectives

Make sure the purpose of your customer interviews is to learn the VOC. It is not a trouble-shooting visit or a sales visit. A good objective statement starts with a verb followed by a phrase that describes the business goals, such as segmenting the market, spotting opportunities, or targeting specific kinds of customers. Use verbs that are useful and clear such as "identify," "define," "describe," "explore," and "generate." A good example of an objective statement is, "Identify and describe key segments based on common benefits. Define criteria for success in each segment."

Step 2. Select Customers to Visit

There are several steps to go through to select customers to visit. First, review your segmentation scheme to understand which customers are in your targeted market segments. Second, in the selected segment, select a few types of customers to visit. Third, select customers in each of the selected type. These should include your current customers and their customers; the customers who expressed an interest in buying your product, but who ultimately bought from your competitors (lost lead); your previous customers who have stopped buying from you (lapsed customers); the potential customers who are ahead of the product curve (power customers); your competitors' customers; and your channel partners. Finally, select people in each customer's organization to interview. To help with this step, draw a buying process chart in that organization and identify people who play roles in that process.

Step 3: Compose the Interview Team

Your interview team should consist of people who have to use the customer information to be gathered by the interview. Make sure the team has people from different business functions. A typical team has three members and each of them play a specific role in the interview. Moderator: The moderator leads the team. This person asks most of questions and keeps the interview on track with the discussion guide. Listener: The listener is responsible for taking thorough notes on the content of interview. Observer: The observer absorbs the total communication presented by the customer and thinks creatively about what is being said.

Step 4: Develop the Discussion Guide

A discussion guide serves as the agenda for the interviews. It covers the content, the sequence, the priority level of topics, and time of the interviews. It also contains questions under each topic for the team to ask customers. Design these questions to identify customers' task demands, to understand the products' context, to identify unsolved problems, and to identify customers' likes and dislikes. Some of your questions should force trade-offs and push for priority among customers' wants.

Step 5: Conduct Interviews

A typical customer interview lasts between one and two hours and it can be divided into three parts: the opening, the middle, and the close. In the opening, ask straightforward and easy questions to build a working relationship with customers. In the middle, ask most of your prepared questions to gather information you need. Give five to ten minutes at the end of interview (the close) in which you ask customers if there is anything else they would like to say on the topics discussed. During the interview, the moderator should ask probing questions when customers' answers are opaque, difficult to follow, or uncertain in their implications. Keep digging until you understand clearly what customers mean. It is important for the moderator to use verbal and body language to quickly establish rapport with customers. The listener should grasp and retain the specificity of customers' answers. The listener should stay alert to context, integrate different remarks into a global perspective, and recognize and retain the range and depth of customer responses. The observer should contemplate the implications of customer statements, integrate and conceptualize all customers' responses into frameworks or models.

Step 6: Debrief after Each Interview

Conduct a debriefing session immediately after the interview. Debriefing gives the team an opportunity to refine the discussion guide and their interview skills, to discover patterns or themes from all the interviews conducted and ensure all team members are on the same page with respect to the interview report.

Step 7: Analyze Interview Data

The VOC data gathered should be analyzed with a variety of tools to make conclusions about customers' needs and wants. Those tools, such as the affinity diagram, the Kano model, conjoint analysis, and quality function deployment, will be discussed in detail in chapter 10.

OTHER METHODS

Focus Groups

Hold a focus group for your customers of a segment to come together to discuss what they need and want. Through observing participants' interaction, attitudes, feelings, and behavior, you will gain deep insight on the requirements and priorities of each customer segment. Conduct at least three focus groups for each customer segment to ensure you have enough and representative data.[3]

Surveys

Conduct surveys to collect information from a large population of your industrial customers. Use the survey data to verify and prioritize the VOC data collected from customer interviews and from focus groups. This method has its pros and cons as compared to other two methods. Survey data is usually quantitative and can be processed easily, but it may not be as accurate in reflecting customers' true feelings. The sample size of your surveys will largely determine the surveys' cost. Use the four factors to determine your sample size: the type of data (discrete or continuous), the purpose of your survey (describing characteristics or comparing groups), estimated standard deviation, and your confidence interval. Survey questions should be specific, without ambiguity. They should provide participants with specific options or scales. Besides a set of multiple-choice questions, include some open-ended questions for customers to freely express their opinions and feelings. Code the survey answers with a predetermined method for data analysis.[3]

VOC FROM IOT CONSUMERS

VOC collection from IoT consumers is somewhat different from industrial VOC collection, but some methods described above can be used for both.[4]

ACTORS AND STAKEHOLDERS

To design your IoT products successfully for a broad range of consumers, start your VOC data collection with actors—the people who will physically handle your products— and stakeholders—the organizations or individuals who don't use your products directly, but have a great interest or concern on the products.

Actors

Actors are either buyers and users or both. Buyers are the customers who make decisions to purchase the product and users are people who interact with the product every day or technicians who install, maintain, and repair the product. Parents who buy video games for their children is a typical example of relationship between buyers and users.

Common questions for customers/buyers are:

1. Why do you want to buy this product?

2. What makes it better than competitors' products?

3. Is it worth the cost?

Common questions for users are:

1. Why do you want this product?

2. What do you want from it?

3. How do you use it?

4. Is it easy for someone like you to use?

5. Will using it change how other people think of you?

Common questions for technicians are:

1. How do you diagnose problems associated with this type of product?

2. What resources (e.g. information, tools, and skills) do you need to fix them?

Stakeholders

Stakeholders affect how a product work. They are indirectly affected by its use. For example, police officers do not own the home security systems, but how quickly they respond to alarms affect how the systems work, and the alarms generated by the systems affect the work and life of the police officers. Keeping stakeholders' interests in mind is very critical to the success of your IoT product design.

THE CONTEXT OF INTERACTION

External factors that affect a product's use always matter to your IoT product design. Look at those factors from four contests:

operational, behavioral, sociocultural, and ecological. Operational Contest The operational contest is the physical world in which an IoT product is used. That includes environmental conditions and some special arrangements. Some questions to study the operational contest are:

1. What environmental conditions might the product encounter?

2. What sorts of resources will likely be available to keep the product functioning?

Behavioral Contest

The behavioral contest includes factors of human activities such as time and place, proximity and visibility, and states of beings such as vision, hearing, or other physiological capacities. These factors play an important role in an IoT product functioning. Some questions to study the behavioral contest are:

1. What kinds of activities are important to you?

2. What tangible attributes characterize those activities?

Sociocultural Contest

How an IoT product functions is also affected by the shared values of the society in which the product is used. Some questions to study the sociocultural contest are:

1. What expectations might actors and stakeholders have for themselves and for the product?

2. What happens when those expectations are violated?

3. How the shared values are created?

Ecological Contest

The ecological contest is about the product ecosystem—the networks of organizational, legal, and economic relationships. Some questions to study the ecological contest are:

1. What actors and stakeholders are involved in creating and maintaining an IoT product?

2. What do they need to participate and cooperate?

VOC DATA COLLECTION TECHNIQUES

You can gather IoT VOC through asking, watching, and making and playing.

Asking

When you ask consumer questions, you gather information that are explainable. Use special maps, timelines, diaries, and usage logs to elicit rich and detailed information.

Spatial maps link consumers' everyday activities to places they are in. They help you see "a network of spaces, with a relationship to each other."[5]

Timelines illustrate the detailed activities of a past event along a timeline. They help consumers tell more detailed and concrete stories.

Diaries and usage logs record what consumers do, think, and feel when they are using the IoT products at the time when you are not around. Those chronicle updates are less biased than retrospective recording.

Watching

When you watch how consumers use your products, you gather the information that are observable. This is usually accomplished through field visits. There are many ways to collect data from a field visit, including:

1. Touring an entire space

2. Observing a person as she is performing an activity

3. Watching all the activities in one specific place

4. Tracing the relationships of activities to document factors that are not easy to articulate

5. Provoking unexpected encounters

Making and Playing

When you have your consumers make and play with your products, you gather tacit information on consumers' everyday needs and wants, as well as how a new product should look, feel, and function. This is usually accomplished through some generative methods such as co-design workshops in which consumers are involved in designing new products by themselves. They put together basic components to make artifacts that surface values, dreams, and assumptions that are usually difficult for consumers to articulate.[4]

Again, analysis of VOC data will be discussed in chapter 10.

CHAPTER FOUR

HOW ARE YOU DOING?

To IoTize your company, you need to understand where you are today and where you want to be in the future, and then develop a plan to move from the current state to the future state.

The best way to understand where your company is today from the IoT perspective is to identify your current business models for every major market segment that you are serving. Identifying your business models requires a good understanding of your current business processes through process mapping. Combining your knowledge on your current state and your current business environment which will be discussed in the next chapter, you will be able to figure out the strengths and weaknesses of your company, as well as the opportunities and threats your company is facing.

IDENTIFYING BUSINESS MODELS

Your business models describe the rationales of how your company creates, delivers, and captures value. Use the business model canvas developed by Alexander Osterwalder and Yves Pigneur for this purpose,[1] a technique adopted by European Platforms Initiative on IoT and other members of the IoT communities.[2-5] The template of the canvas is shown in Figure 4.0.[1]

The business model canvas consists of nine components: customer segments, value propositions, channels, customer relationships, revenue streams, key resources, key activities, key partnerships, and cost structure.

Key Partners	Key Activities	Value Propositions	Customer Relationships	Customer Segments
	Key Resources		Channels	
Cost Structure			Revenue Streams	

Fig. 4.0: Template of the Business Model Canvas

CUSTOMER SEGMENTS

The component of customer segments defines the different groups of your customers. You will need to identify your business model for each of your major customer segments. Table 4.0 summarizes common types of customer segments.

VALUE PROPOSITIONS

The component of value propositions describes the bundle of products and services that create value for the identified customer segment. Table 4.1 lists major elements of value proposition.

Customer Segment Type	Description
Mass market	A large group of customers with broadly similar needs and problems
Niche Market	A group of customers with specific requirements of a niche market
Segmented	A group of customers between market segments with slightly different needs and problems
Diversified	A group of customers belonging to several unrelated customer segments with very different needs and problems
Multisided	A group of customers belonging to multiple interdependent customer segments

Table 4.0: Common Types of Customer Segments

Value Proposition Element	Source of Value
Newness	New-to-the-market products or services
Performance	Improved product or service performance
Customization	Tailored products and services that satisfy the customer's specific needs
"Getting the job down"	Products or services that help a customer get certain jobs down
Design	Products or services with a superior design
Brand/Status	Products or services with a specific brand
Price	Low price

Table 4.1: Major Components of Vale Proposition

CHANNELS

The component of channels describes how your company reaches and communicates with identified customer segments to deliver your value proposition. Table 4.2 summarizes the common types of channels.

Channel type	Description
Own direct	Salesforce, web sales
Own indirect	Own stores
Shared	Partner stores, wholesaler

Table 4.2: Common Types of Channels

CUSTOMER RELATIONSHIPS

The component of customer relationships describes the types of your company's relationships with the identified customer segment. Table 4.3 shows the major categories of customer relationships.

Customer Relationship	Description
Personal assistance	A customer representative communicates and helps customer by variety of means
Dedicated personal assistance	A dedicated customer representative helps an individual client
Self-service	Companies provide means for customers to help themselves
Automated service	Companies provide customers with automated services
Communities	Companies facilitate connections between community members
Co-creation	Companies co-create values with customers

Table 4.3: Major Categories of Customer Relationships

REVENUE STREAMS

The component of revenue streams represents the cash your company generates from the identified customer segment. Table 4.4 summarizes the ways to generate revenue streams.

KEY RESOURCES

The component of key resources describes the most important assets needed for the success of the business model. Table 4.5 summarizes the categories of key resources.

Way to Generate Revenue Streams	Description
Asset sale	Selling ownership rights to a physical product
Usage fee	Selling the right use of a particular service
Subscription fees	Selling continuous access to a service
lending/renting/ leasing	Selling the right to use a particular asset for a fixed period
Licensing	Selling the right to use protected intellectual property
Brokerage fees	Selling intermediation services performed on behalf of multiple parties
Advertising	Selling the right for advertising a particular product, service, or brand

Table 4.4: Ways to Generate Revenue Streams

Key Resource Type	Description
Physical	Physical assets such as manufacturing facilities, buildings, vehicles, machines, systems, point-of-sales systems, and distribution networks
Intellectual	Brands, proprietary knowledge, patents and copyrights, partnerships, and customer databases
Human	People
Financial	Cash, lines of credit, or a stock option pool for hiring key employees

Table 4.5: Types of Key Resources

KEY ACTIVITES

The component of key activities describes the most important activities your company must do for the success of the business model. Table 4.6 summarizes the categories of key activities.

Key Activity Type	Description
Production	Designing, making, and delivering a product
Problem solving	Coming up with new solutions to individual customers
Platform/network	Networks, matchmaking, platforms, software, and brands

Table 4.6: Categories of Key Activities

KEY PARTNERSHIPS

The component of key partnerships describes the network of suppliers and partners needed for the success of the business model. Companies are motivated to create partnerships by optimization and economy scale, by reduction of risk and uncertainty, or by acquisition of specific resources and activities.

COST STRUCTURE

The component of cost structure describes all costs incurred to operate the business model. Business model cost structures can be either cost-driven or value-driven. Cost-driven business models focus on minimizing costs, while value-driven business models focus on value creation. The business model design process has five phases: mobilize, understand, design, implement, and manage, which will be described in detail in chapter 7.

BUSINESS MODEL CANVAS FOR IOT MICROPROCESSOR DESIGN

Arm Holdings is a multinational semiconductor and software design company. Its primary business is in the design ARM processors (CPUs) used in all classes of computing devices. Unlike most traditional microprocessor suppliers, Arm only creates and licenses its technology as intellectual property, rather than making and selling physical products. Figure 4.1 is Arm's business model for its microprocessor design business.[4]

Key Partners	Key Activities	Value Propositions	Customer Relationships	Customer Segments
1. Cooperation with three manufactures to produce the microprocessors we designed 2. Cooperation with approximately ten software developing companies to operate the microprocessors	1. Design of microprocessors 2. Sale of the design to the manufactures **Key Resources** 1. Worldwide four thousand employees 2. Majority of employees has minimum two degrees in computer engineering	1. Limit the energy use of the microprocessor design 2. Include security from the start of the design and offer the same level of security as in banking products 3. USP: design and sell software that helps the chip manufactures deliver the best quality products	Discuss with our customers and their customers to understand how their products/services will look like in three to four years **Channels** Optimize the design of the microprocessors via direct contact with the customers and their customers	1. Three manufactures who produce microprocessors for various customers in various segments 2. Our customers' customers: 2.1 Smartphones (Samsung, Apple, Nokia, Huawei) 2.2. IoT products (connected cars, sensors, embedded functions, etc.)

Cost Structure	Revenue Streams
Main cost comes from resources - our four thousand employees	1. License fees from the sale of our design 2. Occasional grants in EU and USA

Fig. 4.1: Arm's Business Model for Its Microprocessor Design Business

MATCHING BUSINESS MODEL PATTERNS

Patterns of business models are the similar characteristics and behavior of business models. Matching your business models with the common patterns forces you to recognize the characteristics and behavior your business models share with other business models and realize which patterns your future business models will match when you develop your business strategies to IoTize your company.

GENERAL BUSINESS MODEL PATTERNS

Five general business patterns are listed in Table 4.7: unbundling business models, the long-tail, multisided platforms, FREE as a business model, and open business models.1 After you have identified your business models, look at the patterns of business models listed in Table 4.7 and ask yourself if your business models fit in any of these patterns.

Arm's business model, for example, fits in the pattern of the long tail in the general business model pattern categories.

Pattern	Description	Requirement
Unbundling business models	Unbundle three coexist types of businesses: customer relationship, Customer intimacy, and operational excellence	Separate different types of businesses to avoid conflicts or undesirable tradeoffs
The long tail	Offer a larger number of small-volume niche products	Maintain low inventory costs and strong platforms
Multisided platforms	Bring together multiple groups of customers by facilitating interactions between the customer groups	Deliver value to one customer group only if other customer groups are also present
FREE as a business model	Offer at least one customer segment with free-of-charge products or services	Non-paying customers are financed by another part of the business model or by another customer segment
Open business models	Collaborate with outside partners to create and capture value	Exploit external ideas within the company or provide external parties with ideas or assets

Table 4.7: Patterns of General Business Models

IOT BUSINESS MODEL PATTERNS

If you are already in the IoT world, you need to check if your business models fit in any of the IoT business patterns.

There are six IoT business patterns that follow the IoT value chain, ranging from consumer-facing business models to industry-facing business models, as shown in Figure 4.2.[4]

Fig. 4.2: IoT Business Model Patterns

1. Modular hardware solutions: This business model pattern is related to the hardware layer—the layer that provides the essential capabilities of signal capture, data generation, data transmission, and actuation. The business models in this pattern focus on intercommunication and interoperability of parts to maximize usability, design of the right infrastructure for specific use case, and the architecture, implementation, and maintenance of hardware.

2. Virtual asset sharing: Business models in this pattern focus on distributed asset consolidation and capacity sharing to minimize downtime and to generate recurring revenue stream for the original investors in the assets. The most common example is the cloud service providers who consolidate their servers and rent their unused processing power via timeshare to empower an entire ecosystem of users.

3. Data storage and brokerage: The business models in this pattern focus on data management service by assuring the safe data storage transmission, and by providing add-on services such as data munging/structuring and data borage, that is, selling anonymized data and paying third parties with corresponding royalties and data generators.

4. Data analytics and insights: The business models in this pattern focus on data analytics as a service by analyzing data to support decision making, and by conducting machine learning for smart optimization, customization, or personalization.

5. Dynamic data bundling: The business models in this pattern focus on data curation services by combining relevant data streams from various sources and providing the bundled data to end users.

6. Dematerialized data feeds: Business models in this pattern focus on timeshare rental and microtransactions by providing the dematerialized data feeds to end users through APIs and simple pay-as-you-go pricing model.

Arm's business model, for example, fits in the pattern of modular hardware solutions of the IoT business model pattern categories.

BUSINESS MODEL PATTERN MATRIX

To understand the position of your business model in both general business model patterns and in the IoT business model patters, make a business model pattern matrix by listing the general business patterns on the first column and listing the IoT business patterns in the first row, as shown in Table 4.8. Positioning your business model in this matrix allows you to understand how your company creates, delivers, and captures value in both the traditional business world and in the IoT world. It helps you think creatively about how to improve your business to create more value for your customers.

		IoT BM Patterns					
		Modular hardware solutions	Virtual asset sharing	Data storage and brokerage	Data analytics and insights	Dynamic data bundling	Demater- ialized data feeds
General BM Patterns	Unbundling business models						
	The long tail						
	Multisided platforms						
	FREE as a business model						
	Open business models						

Table 4.8: Business Model Pattern Matrix Table 4.9 shows the position of Arm's business model in the matrix.

		IoT BM Patterns					
		Modular hardware solutions	Virtual asset sharing	Data storage and brokerage	Data analytics and insights	Dynamic data bundling	Demater-ialized data feeds
General BM Patterns	Unbundling business models						
	The long tail	X					
	Multisided platforms						
	FREE as a business model						
	Open business models						

Table 4.9: Arm's Business Model in the Business Model Pattern Matrix

PROCESS MAPPING

To develop your business models, you need to understand your business processes well. You can describe your company as a set of business processes, and each of them provides products and service to its internal or external customers, adding value for them.

Mapping your business processes is the best way to understand them.[6] To start, draw an organizational process map at the highest level, as illustrated in Fig. 4.3, a process overview map for a company making silicon wafers in the semiconductor industry. Start with your supplier, go through your internal process step, and end with your customers who receives your products. The work-level process maps help you identify customer-supplier relationships, flow of information and material, and potential "disconnects"—the necessary connection is either broken or does not exist.

After you have accurately developed the process overview map, map your business process for each of the major steps in your process overview map. Figure 4.4 is a process map for the final cleaning step in Figure 4.3.

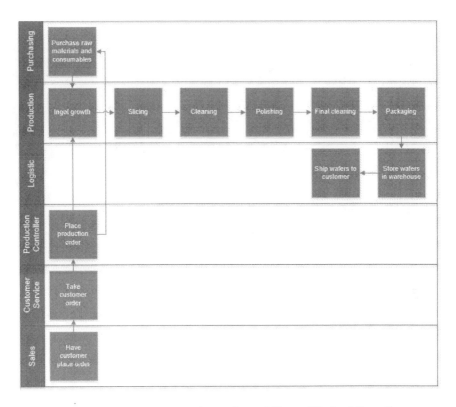

Fig. 4.3: Process Overview Map for a Silicon Wafer Manufacture

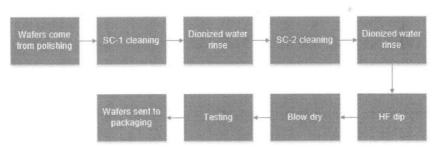

Fig. 4.4: Process Map for the Final Cleaning Step in Figure 4.3

PROCESS MAPPING FOR IOT MAILING

In chapter 2, we discussed an IoT application in mailing. Let's review the case.

Pitney Bowes, a provider of postage, mailing, shipping products, and solutions, applies the IoT solution to create business value for its large-scale printing and mailing business. The company embedded hundreds of sensors on its inserters in the printing and mailing equipment that the company sells to its customers. The sensors send process data to local computers which are connected to the Internet through a Cisco 819 Integrated Service Router. Data then is transferred through the transport layer security (TLS) connection and then collected by GE's Predix platform. GE's analytics services perform data analysis through configuration, abstraction, and extensible modules. Through continuously monitoring inserters and issuing pre-failure alert, the IoT solution has significantly improved service quality and reduce the service cost. Once an alarm appears that indicates a potential failure on an equipment at a customer site, service technicians will arrive there with the correct parts. With a large database that continuously receiving data from customers, Pitney Bowes is developing benchmarks to help customers improve their productivity.[7]

Figure 4.5 shows the process of Pitney Bowes IoT mailing solution.

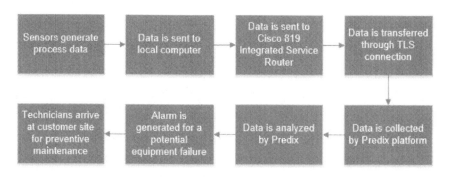

Fig. 4.5: Process Map for IoT Mailing Solution

SWOT ANALYSIS

With information gathered from studies on VOC, your current situation and your external analysis (see next chapter), put them together to figure out the strengths and weaknesses of your company, and the opportunities and threats that your company is facing. This activity is called SWOT analysis. SWOT stands for strengths, weaknesses, opportunities, and threats. By performing a SWOT analysis, you conduct an internal scan of your company based on its strengths and weaknesses, and external scan based on the opportunities and threats it is facing. Use the affinity diagram, the tool described in detail in chapter 10, to construct the SWOT diagram. A SWOT analysis provides your leadership team with critical information for developing your business vision and strategies that will discussed in the part 2 of this book.

The Tesla SWOT analysis shown in Fig. 4.6 is intriguing.[8] Tesla is a strong innovative company, but it has booked operating losses almost every year since its initial public offering. The SWOT analysis demonstrates that Tesla's greatest strength—innovation—comes with prices of high costs and low market readiness. The huge potential of electrical car market attracts severe global competition. Therefore, Tesla's management team needs to maintain sustainable funding avenues and be innovative not only on product features, but also on cutting operational costs as well.

Strengths	Weaknesses
Well-known CEO with good track record	CEO is also CEO/CTO of SpaceX
Uses Telsa Stores instead of traditional distribution through dealers	Infrastructure not yet developed for electric cars
First company to produce a fully electric luxury car	Customers are still wary of such new innovations
Based in SF Bay area	Price
Popular in younger age groups who are likely to use social media	
Opportunities	Threats
Increasing awareness and support for environmentalism	Competition from established auto companies
Large international market potential	Lawsuits could inhibit/delay innovations
New lower-price models appealing to a wider range of customers	Loss of government subsidies will drive up prices
Advances in tech may increase battery life; spark other innovations	

Fig. 4.6: SWOT Diagram for Tesla Motor Company

CHAPTER FIVE

WHAT IS YOUR BUSINESS ENVIRONMENT?

One of the challenges that you as an entrepreneur face is to understand the business environment that your company is in, that is, how your competitors are doing, what are the best practices your company can learn from, and what are some most important external factors that could affect your business. This chapter will discuss the tools for this purpose: competitive analysis, benchmarking, and STEEP analysis.

COMPETITIVE ANALYSIS

Knowing who your competitors are and how they are doing is a critical part of your strategic planning. It helps you understand how competitive your products are as compared to your competitors'. The following is the general procedure for conducting a good competitive analysis:

1. Set measurement metrics.

2. Choose your major customer segments.

3. For each chose customer segment, identify major competitors.

4. Collect data for each identified competitor.

5. Analyze these competitors' business models.

6. Compare competitors' business models and performance with yours.

7. If the competitors' performance is better than yours, find your gaps and possible root causes.

MEASUREMENT METRICS

Measurement metrics are a set of measurements to gauge the performance of a function, operation, or business through various financial and nonfinancial performance indicators.[1] Some common financial performance indicators are cash flow, revenue, cost, and return on investment. Quality, delivery, new product launches, health, and safety are some common nonfinancial performance indicators.

CUSTOMER SEGMENTS

To start, choose the major customer segments that your company is serving. You have done this work in your internal analysis in chapter 4. Recall that there are five common types of customer segments: mass market, niche market, segmented, diversified, and multisided segments (Table 5.0).

Customer Segment Type	Description
Mass market	A large group of customers with broadly similar needs and problems
Niche Market	A group of customers with specific requirements of a niche market
Segmented	A group of customers between market segments with slightly different needs and problems
Diversified	A group of customers belonging to several unrelated customer segments with very different needs and problems
Multisided	A group of customers belonging to multiple interdependent customer segments

Table 5.0: Common Types of Customer Segments

MAJOR COMPETITORS

For each chosen customer segment, identify major competitors in the segment. There are basically two types of competitors in the IoT world: the existing competitors and the future competitors. Consider both when you are choosing your competitors to analyze.

Existing Competitors

Existing competitors are the companies that your company is competing with today. Some of them may have gained some advantages over you by entering the IoT earlier than you, but most of them are probably like you: they do not have inherent IoT competitive advantages to begin with.

Future Competitors

These are the companies who will be your competitors when you eventually get in the IoT world. They will not only compete with your products, but also compete with your business ecosystems. The future competition will also come from the software companies that do not have physical products currently, but they have software and data science and they may equip physical products with software and data science to enter the ecosystem quickly in the future. Find out who they are, what they are doing, and what they plan to do in the future.[2]

DATA COLLETION

Collect data for your competitive analysis from the following resources:[1, 3, 4]

1. Trade association's studies and libraries

2. University research services

3. Department of Commerce

4. Industry consultants

5. IoT subject matter experts

6. American Productivity & Quality Center (APQC)
   (https://www.apqc.org/)

7. APQC Portal (https://www.apqc.org/benchmarking-portal/)

8. The Benchmarking Exchange (http://www.benchnet.com/)

9. Best Practice, LLC & Global Benchmarking Council
   (https://www.best-in-class.com/)

10. SEMrush (https://www.semrush.com/)

11. Baldrige Performance Excellence Program
    (https://www.nist.gov/baldrige/)

BUSINESS MODELS

For each identified competitor, analyze its business model using the business model canvas.[5] As described in chapter 4, the business model canvas consists of nine components: customer segments, value propositions, channels, customer relationships, revenue streams, key resources, key activities, key partnerships, and cost structure (Figure 5.0).

Key Partners	Key Activities	Value Propositions	Customer Relationships	Customer Segments
	Key Resources		**Channels**	
Cost Structure		**Revenue Streams**		

Fig. 5.0: Template of the Business Model Canvas

After you have analyzed the business model of your competitor, determine which pattern of general business models (Table 5.1) your competitor's business model matches, and which pattern of IoT business models (Figure 5.1) it fits. Put your competitor's business model in the business model matrix (Table 5.2).

Pattern	Description	Requirement
Unbundling business models	Unbundle three coexist types of businesses: customer relationship, Customer intimacy, and operational excellence	Separate different types of businesses to avoid conflicts or undesirable tradeoffs
The long tail	Offer a larger number of small-volume niche products	Maintain low inventory costs and strong platforms
Multisided platforms	Bring together multiple groups of customers by facilitating interactions between the customer groups	Deliver value to one customer group only if other customer groups are also present
FREE as a business model	Offer at least one customer segment with free-of-charge products or services	Non-paying customers are financed by another part of the business model or by another customer segment
Open business models	Collaborate with outside partners to create and capture value	Exploit external ideas within the company or provide external parties with ideas or assets

Table 5.1: Patterns of General Business Models

Fig. 5.1: IoT Business Model Patterns

	IoT BM Patterns					
	Modular hardware solutions	Virtual asset sharing	Data storage and brokerage	Data analytics and insights	Dynamic data bundling	Demater-ialized data feeds
General BM Patterns Unbundling business models						
The long tail						
Multisided platforms						
FREE as a business model						
Open business models						

Table 5.2: Business Model Pattern Matrix

BUSINESS MODEL AND PERFORMANCE COMPARISON

Compare your competitors' business models and their performance with yours and compile the information into a template shown in Table 5.3.

Company	Customer Segments	Value Propositions	Channels	Customer Relationships	Revenue Streams	Key Resources
Competitor						
Our Company						

Company	Key Activities	Key Partnerships	Cost Structures	Business Model Patterns	Financial Performance Indicators	Nonfinancial Performance Indicators
Competitor						
Our Company						

Table 5.3: Template for Business Model and Performance Comparison

GAP ANALYSIS

If the competitor's performances are better than yours, find the gaps and investigate possible root causes.

BENCHMARKING

Benchmarking is a technique used to search for best business practices that lead to superior performance. It is "a process for rigorously measuring your performance versus the best-in-class companies and for using the analysis to meet and surpass the best-in-class," as defined by Kaiser Associates, a management consulting firm that has actively promoted benchmarking.[1] Benchmarking, if performed systematically, will spur extraordinary insights and breakthrough thinking; it will help your company accelerate your business improvement.

THREE TYPES OF BENCHMARKING

There are three primary benchmarking types: process benchmarking, performance benchmarking, and strategic benchmarking.[1]

Process Benchmarking

Process benchmarking focuses on discrete business processes, such as a manufacturing process, a product development process, or a customer service process.

Performance Benchmarking

Performance benchmarking focuses on performance of your products by comparing its competitive elements such as price, quality, and delivery with that of your competitors' products.

Strategic Benchmarking

Strategic benchmarking focuses on the comparison of your company's completeness with the best-in-industry or best-in-world performers. Perform strategic benchmarking for your company's IoTization mission.

BENCHMARKING PROCEDURE

The general procedure below for conducting a good benchmarking is the same as the procedure for competitive analysis, except that you choose the best-in-class to study instead of your competitors.

1. Set measurement metrics.

2. Identify a best-in-class company.

3. Collect data for the best-in-class company.

4. Analyze this company's business model.

5. Compare the best performer's business model and performance with yours.

6. Find your gaps and investigate the possible root causes.

STEEP ANALYSIS

Business leaders today are all under tremendous pressure to deliver quick results. They tend to make quick decisions before carefully studying the situation. STEEP analysis helps them get a detailed overview on the external factors that are forming the trends and may cause something to happen in the future.

STEEP FACTORS

STEEP stands for social, technological, economic, environmental, and political. These factors affect the environment in which your company operates.

Social Factors

The social factors include consumer behavior, demographics, crime rate, religion, lifestyles, value conceptions, and social media.

Technological Factors

The technical factors significantly affect technological advancement, such as innovation, research and development, technology advancement in key areas, patent regulations, and life cycle of products.

Economic Factors

The economic factors that heavily affect economic growth include debt and deficit of federal and local government, governmental monetary and fiscal policies, interest rate, currency exchange rate, stock and bond market, job market, unemployment rate, productivity growth, international trade, taxes, inflation, average personal saving and debt level, inflation, and subsidies.

Environmental factors

Environmental factors include global warming, water resources, natural disasters, food, soil, pollution, and environmental regulations.

Political factors

Political factors affect relationships between countries, parties, organizations, and individuals. They include trust in governments, income inequality, social division, political parties, governmental regulations and policies, jurisdiction, and trade unions.[6]

STEEP ANALYSIS PROCEDURE A good STEEP analysis typically involves a five-step process.[6]

1. Understand the STEEP factors. Collect and analyze data to comprehend the trends and events of STEEP factors in terms of their nature and their evolving histories.

2. Assess the interrelationships between different trends. Reveal the interactions between the trends, that is, their positive or negative effects on each other and the magnitude of those effects.

3. Forecast the direction of the trends. Identify the cause and signs of the trends to find the driven forces behind them. This will give you good information on where these trends are heading.

4. Relate the trends to your business. Understand how these trends will influence your company's business. Predict as best as you can on what trends will affect your business, what effects they will have, how they will affect you, as well as the time and location these effects will take place.

5. Derive the implications. Summarize the implications of your study, make conclusions, and recommend actions to your business leaders.

CONTINUITY

After the study, keep your business leaders informed on the changes of the STEEP factors, educating them through seminars or a self-study organized by internal or external experts. Collaborate with consultants or universities to charter a special research project on a high risk, but large opportunity indicated by the STEEP trends. Invite your executives to participate in some customer visits so they understand the possible future developments and trends from the customers' point of view.[3]

PART THREE

FUTURE STATE

The best way to predict future is to invent it.

— Alan Kay

CHAPTER SIX

WHERE DO YOU WANT TO BE?

In part 2, you have collected and analyzed a lot of data about your company and your business environment—your current state. Now you want to know where you want to be —your future state. Moving toward a desired future state starts with a vision, followed by creating business objectives and strategies.

STRATEGIC VISION

A vision is a statement of the future state of your company. It sets the direction and creates a context for prioritization of your strategies and objectives. A shared vision will inspire all the people in your company to strive to arrive at the desired goal.[1]

The famous story of President Kennedy and a NASA janitor illustrate the power of an inspiring vision. During a visit to a NASA Space Center in 1962, President John F. Kennedy saw a janitor carrying a broom. He walked over to the janitor and said, "Hi, I'm Jack Kennedy. What are you doing?" "Well, Mr. President," the man responded, "I'm helping put a man on the moon." The janitor was inspired by NASA's vision and he attached what he was doing every day to that vision.[2]

GOOD VISION STATEMENTS

Your vision statement can be either short or long, depending on your company's culture. Google's vision statement has only one sentence: "To provide access to the world's information in one click." Google's vision statement reflects the company's core business—the search engine service that allows people around the world to easily access information. There are three core parts in Google's vision statement: information, access, and one click. Information is available on numerous services supported by Google's cloud platform. Accessibility is achieved by Google's search engine services available to anyone in the world. The one-click component is fulfilled by the company's innovative products, such as the easy-to-use Google search.[3]

Another short example of a vision statement is Amazon's: "Our vision is to be earth's most customer-centric company, to build a place where people can come to find and discover anything they might want to buy online."[4]

Apple's current vision statement was introduced by its CEO Tim Cook, who stated, "We believe that we are on the face of the earth to make great products and that's not changing. We are constantly focusing on innovating. We believe in the simple, not the complex. We believe that we need to own and control the primary technologies behind the products that we make and participate only in markets where we can make a significant contribution. We believe in saying no to thousands of projects, so that we can really focus on the few that are truly important and meaningful to us. We believe in deep collaboration and cross-pollination of our groups, which allow us to innovate in a way that others cannot. And frankly, we don't settle for anything less than excellence in every group in the company, and we have the self-honesty to admit when we're wrong and the courage to change. And I think regardless of who is in what job, those values are so embedded in this company that Apple will do extremely well."

Apple's long vision statement reflects the company's business practice and culture. It emphasizes innovation, specifies simplicity, indicates careful selection of markets, and highlights employees' collaboration and excellence. Such a detailed vision statement guides the company's leaders and employees in working toward the desired future.[4]

DEVELOPING A VISION STATEMENT

There are six steps involved in the process of creating a vision statement, as shown in Figure 6.0.[1]

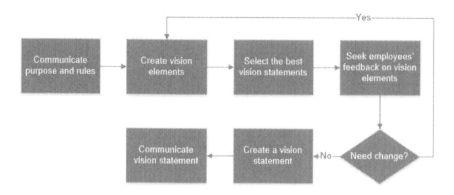

Fig. 6.0: Process for Creating a Vision Statement

Communicate Purpose and Rules

At the beginning of the process of developing your vision, the head of your leadership team must communicate the purpose of the vision development, explaining what the vison is and the reasons for having it; then set ground rules that will guide team members' behavior in order to ensure the effectiveness of the process. Your company's vision is not a product of your CEO, it should be the results of your leadership team's integrated thinking.

Create Vision Elements

The second step is to create a list of vision elements upon which your vision statement will be created. To think about the future, you need to know the present. Review the information collected and analyzed in part 2, including the VOC, your current business models and processes, the analysis of your company's strengths, weaknesses, opportunities, and threats (SWOT), the competitive analysis, benchmarking, and the STEEP analysis. The information review will help you understand your current state— what is working and what is not working or what will not be working soon, and it will help you to come up with a list of good vision elements (Figure 6.1).

After reviewing the present state, the team adapts the divergent think mode to create as many vision elements as possible. Divergent thinking is a type of creative thinking mode that follows many lines of thoughts to generate new and original ideas.5 The common method used in this step is the affinity diagram described in chapter 10.

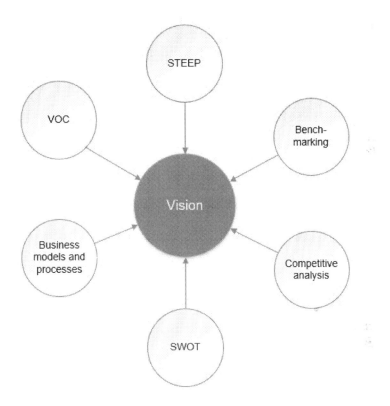

Fig. 6.1: Data Sources for Creating Vision Elements

In this process, all the team members first run a brainstorming session to come up with many vision elements. The most important rule in the brainstorming session is: do not judge any proposed elements at this step because doing so will hinder team members' creative thinking. The team members then organize ideas into some groups based on their commonalities using the affinity diagram. Chapter 10 will describe an application scenario of using the affinity diagram (Fig. 6.2).

Select Vision Elements

Use interrelationship digraph to identify the few most influential vision elements in the overall success—the vision drivers. These vision drivers will be your selected vision elements. How to use the interrelationship digraph will be discussed later in this chapter.

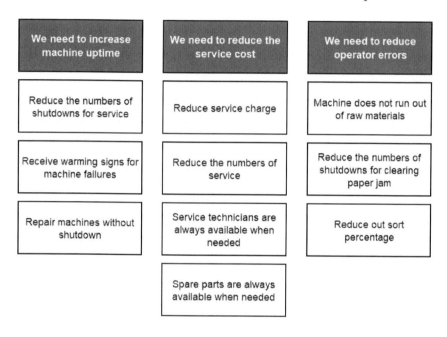

Fig. 6.2: Sample Affinity Diagram

Seek Employees' Feedback

No matter how good you think your vision elements are, they will not be effective and inspiring if there is no buy-in from your employees. To get their buy-in, you must get all the employees involved in the process of creating your vision statement. "No involvement, no commitment," said Dr. Steven Covey, the legendary leadership authority and the author of The Seven Habits of Highly Effective People.[6] Share your vision elements with the entire organization and sincerely seek your employees' feedback. Since IoT is relatively new for many people, hold some training sessions for your employees on what IoT is and why it is important for your business. Otherwise, some employees may not understand where your vision elements come from.

After you have received your employees' feedback, go back to the step of creating vision elements and incorporate the feedback into your vision elements.

Write a Vision Statement

A team member then converts the selected vision elements into a narrative and submits to your team for critics. A good vision statement emerges after several rounds of "refining."

Communicate the Vision Statement In order to hold your vision statement as your "true star" to guide your business planning and execution, broadcast your vision statement. Some communication methods are recommended:

1. A town hall meeting for senior leaders to speak to employees directly on what your vision is and why you need it.

2. Publish the vision statement on your company's Internet and intranet websites.

3. Display it at lobby of your business buildings.

4. Check your business operations periodically to ensure you do not deviate from the path toward your future state stated by your vision.

EXERCISE: DEVELOPING GOOGLE'S VISION STATEMENT

Now let's run an exercise of developing Google's vision statement, applying the above process.

Create Vision Elements

After reviewing the data collected on your present state, your team runs a brainstorming session to come up with many vision elements. Then you organize them into seven categories using the affinity diagram.[7]

1. Ease information access

2. Foster universal education

3. Promote free expression

4. Boost borderless communication

5. Make all information available

6. Stimulate economic globalization

7. Provide one-click products

These seven headers of categories are the vision element candidates. For more information about the affinity diagram, see a real example of its use in chapter 10.

Follow the procedure below to identify the key vision elements using an interrelationship diagraph:

1. Post the seven header cards from the affinity diagram in a circle on a flip chart.

2. Pick an anchor card and compare it to each of the other cards. Draw an arrow from the influencing card to the influenced card if there is a relationship between the two.

3. Repeat step 2 clockwise until all possible pairs have been compared.

4. Count the number of incoming arrows and outgoing arrows for each card. The cards with a high number of outgoing arrows are drivers—the driving force behind the vision. The cards with a high number of incoming arrows are dependents—those that are driven by the drivers. In this case, there are three drivers and they are your key vision elements:

   a. Ease information access.

   b. Make all information available.

c. Develop one-click products.[7]

The rest of the vision element candidates are dependents. The complete interrelation diagraph is shown in Figure 6.3.

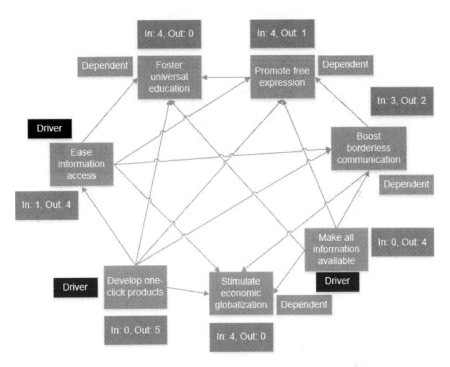

Fig. 6.3: Sample Interrelationship Diagraph Write a Vision Statement

After your employees' feedback has confirmed that the three drivers are the right key vision elements, A team member then converts the selected vision elements into a narrative and submits to your team for critics. The final good vision statement is: "To provide access to the world's information in one click."

STRATEGIC OBJECTIVES

After writing their vison statements, some companies work on all the selected vison elements at the same time. However, if you have resource constraints, this approach will result in diluting your resources, slowing down your progress, making it impossible for your company to act quickly to respond to market and technology changes. Therefore, work on one vision element during any given year and achieve that vision element by the end of the year. This vision element equipped with a set of metrics and targets serves as your strategic objective for the given year.[1] Figure 6.4 depicts the process of setting strategic objectives.

Fig. 6.4: Process of Setting Strategic Objectives

The first step is to correlate your selected vision elements with your major business processes. The second step is to analyze the gaps between your vision elements and your major business processes. At the third step, select a vision element to work on for the given year. Finally, develop business metrics and targets for the selected vision element.

CORRELATE WITH CURRENT PROCESSES

At the first step, you need to understand how well your major business processes support your vision elements. This can be realized by using a matrix that correlates your major business process with your selected vision elements. The format of the matrix is very similar to that of quality function development discussed in chapter 10. List your major processes on the first column of the table and list your vision elements on the first row. Then determine the strength of the link between individual processes and individual vision elements. Assign number 9 to a strong correlation, 3 to a median correlation, and 1 to a weak one. Table 6.0 is a sample correlation matrix.

Process	Vision Element 1	Vision Element 2	Vision Element 3
A	1	3	9
B	3	1	9
C	3	3	3
D	3	9	3

Table 6.0: Sample Correlation Matrix (Vision Elements vs. Processes)

ANALYZE GAPS

After you have a good understanding on the relationship between your major business processes and your vision elements, you want to know how big the gaps between them are. You can accomplish this by using a radar chart. Here is the procedure to draw a radar chart:

1. Select a major business process.

2. Draw a circle called a radar screen.

3. Place your vision elements around the rim of the radar screen.

4. Draw lines from the center of the radar screen to each of the vison elements.

5. Set a scale of 0 to 10 on each line, with 0 on the center of the circle and 10 on the rim. The number 10 represents the full accomplishment on that vision element while number 0 indicates no accomplishment at all.

6. Mark the current state of the businesses processes on the scale of 0-10 for each of the vision elements.[1]

Make a radar chart for every major business process (Figure 6.5). Since no single person in your leadership team can accurately scale your current states of all your major business processes on the radar chart, you need to get your whole team involved on this task.

SELECT A VISION ELEMENT TO WORK ON

With the correlation ratings from step 1 and the gap rating from step 2 for every vision element, you can calculate the total rating of each vision element for every major business process by summing the correlation rating and gap rating, as demonstrated by Table 6.1.

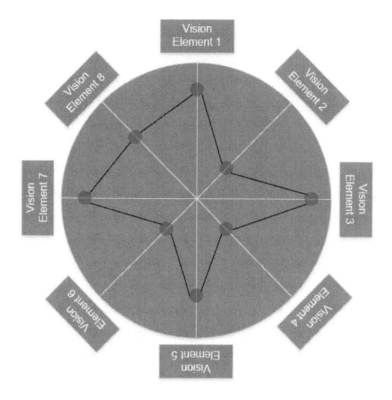

Fig. 6.5: Sample Radar Chart

Process A	Vision Element 1	Vision Element 2	Vision Element 3
Correlation Rating	1	3	9
Gap Rating	4	6	1
Total Rating	5	9	10

Table 6.1: Vision Element Ratings for a Single Business Process

Then sum up the total ratings of all the processes for every vision element to come up with the grant total rating of every vision element for all the processes. For example, if you have four major business processes and you have calculated the total ratings of vision elements for each of the processes, the final rating of a vision element is calculated by summing up the total ratings of every process, as demonstrated by Table 6.2.

Process	Vision Element 1	Vision Element 2	Vision Element 3
A	5	9	10
B	6	12	4
C	20	11	9
D	11	25	4
Grant Total Rating	42	57	27

Table 6.2: Vision Element Ratings for All Major Processes

The vision element with the highest grant total rating is the one you choose to work on for the given year. In this example, it is vision element two.

DEVELOP MEASUREMENT METRICS AND TARGETS

The selected vision element could be a qualitative statement, such as: "Provide customers in automotive industry with IoT solutions." To measure the progress of achieving the vision element in a given year, you need to establish a set of measurement metrics that gauges the performance of your company on the selected vision element through various financial and nonfinancial performance indicators. The elements in your metrics must be tangible, quantitative, and measurable. Like the measurement metrics used in competitive analysis and benchmarking, some common financial performance indicators are cash flow, revenue, cost, and return on investment. Quality, delivery, new product launches, health and safety are some common nonfinancial performance indicators.[8]

After you have established a set of measurement metrics for the selected vision element, set progressive targets for these metrics along with a timeline to ensure that the objective will be achieved at the end of the timeline.

CHAPTER SEVEN

HOW TO DEVELOP IOT STRATEGIES

To achieve the business objective discussed in chapter 6, you need to develop new business strategies at every level of your organization, and you need to revise some of your existing business models.

DEVELOPING HEIRARCHICAL BUSINESS STRATEGIES

Figure 7.0 depicts the process of developing your improvement strategies and sub-strategies.[1]

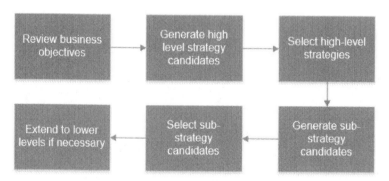

Fig. 7.0: Process for Developing Hierarchical Business Strategies

REVIEW BUSINESS OBJECTIVE

The first thing you want to do is to review the business objective that you are developing your business strategies for. Go back to your vison element to understand why the objective is set and study the metrics that measure the success of the objective.

GENERATE HIGH-LEVEL STRATEGY CANDIDATES At this step, the team adopts the divergent thinking mode to generate as many strategy candidates as possible. Use the affinity diagram tool to organize these ideas into groups based on their commonalities.[2] Figure 7.1 is a sample affinity diagram. The method of constructing an affinity diagram will be described in detail in chapter 10.

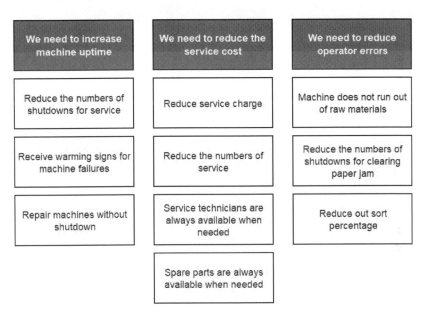

Fig. 7.1: Sample Affinity Diagram

SELECT HIGH-LEVEL STRATEGIES

The team then switches from the divergent thinking mode to the convergent thinking mode to select the best strategies. Use tools such as multivoting or prioritization matrix for the selection purpose. If you have enough information to set clear evaluation criteria, use the prioritization matrix. Otherwise, multivoting is your choice. It is easier to use but is less rigorous than the prioritization matrix.[2]

Multivoting

At each step of the multivoting process, each participant selects a certain number of strategic candidates from the list that should be roughly half of the total number of ideas. At each step of the multivoting process, the candidates that have a low number of votes are eliminated. This process is repeated until a conclusion is reached.

Table 7.0 illustrates the three voting steps participated in by five team members. The green color indicates the candidates chosen at each voting step. On the first vote, each of the five participants selects four candidates from seven candidates, and the three candidates with the fewest votes are eliminated. On the second vote, each participant selects three candidates from four candidates, and two candidates with the most votes remain in the race. On the final vote, each participant chooses one candidate. In this example, all the votes go to strategy candidate four.

Strategy Candidate	1st Vote	2nd Vote	3rd Vote
Strategy candidate 1	0		
Strategy candidate 2	2		
Strategy candidate 3	5	5	
Strategy candidate 4	5	5	5
Strategy candidate 5	4	3	
Strategy candidate 6	1		
Strategy candidate 7	3	2	

Table 7.0: Sample Multivoting Application

Prioritization Matrix

Table 7.1 demonstrates the method of the prioritization matrix. In the process, the team rates three strategy candidates on a one-to-five scale against three criteria, each with a weight. The team multiplies each rating by the weight associated to each criterion to get the score for each candidate under each criterion. All the weighted scores are added to calculate the priority score for each candidate. In this case, the team selects strategy candidate three as the best candidate because it has the highest priority score.

Criterion	Possibility of Success	Cost	Sustainability	Priority Score
Weight	50	25	25	
Strategy Candidate				
Strategy candidate 1	1	5	1	50 x 1 + 25 x 5 + 25 x 1 = 200
Strategy candidate 2	2	3	4	50 x 2 + 25 x 3 + 25 x 4 = 275
Strategy candidate 3	5	1	5	50 x 5 + 25 x 1 + 25 x 5 = 400

Table 7.1: Sample Prioritization Matrix

Now, use a tree diagram to demonstrate the relationships between your business objective and your high-level strategies.[1] The application of a tree diagram will be discussed shortly in this chapter.

EXERCISE: DEVELOPING GOOGLE STRATEGIES

Recall Google's vision statement discussed in chapter 6: "To provide access to the world's information in one click."[3] Based on our analysis, the vision statement has three elements:

1. Ease information access

2. Make all information available

3. Develop one-click products

These elements, each equipped with a set of measurement metrics, will be Google's business objectives. Now let's run an exercise for your team to tackle Google's business objective of making all information available. Following the ideation procedure that we have discussed early, you select two high-level strategies for this objective: provide users with Google services and support these services with the Google cloud platform. The tree diagram reveals the relationship between the objective and your high-level strategies (Figure 7.2).

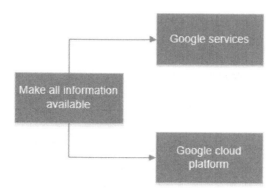

Fig. 7.2: Tree Diagram Relating the Business Objective to the High-Level Strategies

GENERATE SUB-LEVEL STRATEGY CANDIDATES

If your high-level strategies are not granulated enough for the lower levels of your company to implement, your need to develop sub-level strategies. The methodology is the same as the one used for developing your high-level strategies. For each of the high-level strategies, brainstorm as many sub-strategy candidates as possible and then use the affinity diagram to put them into groups according to their commonalities.

SELECT SUB-LEVEL STRATEGIES

Same as what you have done for selecting your high-level strategies, use either multivoting or the prioritization matrix to select best sub-strategies. Repeat this process to develop all sub-strategies for every high-level strategy. Go back to the exercise of developing Google strategies. For each of your high-level strategies, you decide sub-level strategies as shown in Figure 7.3—the tree diagram that clearly demonstrate the relationships between the business objective, the high-level strategies, and the sub-level strategies.

EXTEND THE PROCESS TO LOWER LEVELS IF NECESSARY

Some large companies have a complex, multilevel organizational structure. In that case, extend this process further to the lower levels of the organization.

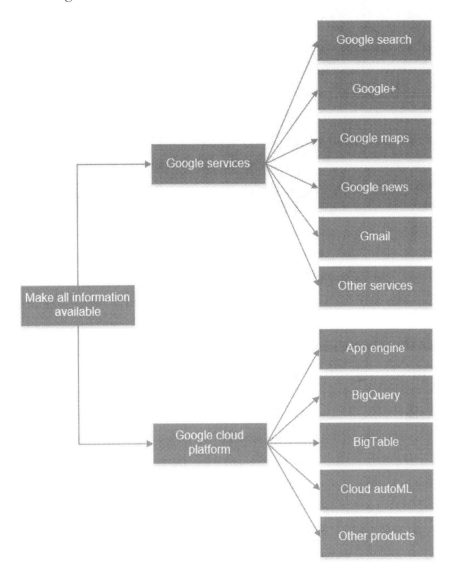

Fig. 7.3: Tree Diagram that Reveals Relationships Between Business Objective, High-Level Strategies, and Sub-Level Strategies

DESIGN IOT BUSINESS MODELS

After you have decided to take the leap on IoTization, you will quickly find out that many of your existing business models no longer work in the IoT world. In chapter 4, we discussed how to discover your current business models for the major customer segments. In this chapter, we will discuss how to design new business models to IoTize your company and your products. Figure 7.4 depicts the five-step process for designing your IoT business models.[4]

Fig. 7.4: Business Model Design Process

MOBILIZE

The objective of this step is to prepare for a successful business model design project. At this step, you assemble a team, develop a project plan, set the project objectives, collect all data needed, and test preliminary ideas.

Use the business model canvas as the tool to describe, design, and analyze business models.[4] Recalling what has been discussed in chapter 4, the business model canvas consists of nine components: customer segments: value propositions, channels, customer relationships, revenue streams, key resources, key activities, key partnerships, and cost structure (Figure 7.5).

UNDERSTAND

At this step, the team researches and analyzes the data collected to understand the context in which the new business model will evolve. Immerse yourselves in the data collected through VOC investigation (chapter 3), your current processes and business models (chapter 4), SWOT analysis (chapter 4), competitive analysis (chapter 5), benchmarking (chapter 5), STEEP analysis (chapter 5), your company's new vision statement and business objective (chapter 6), and your business strategies (this chapter).

Key Partners	Key Activities	Value Propositions	Customer Relationships	Customer Segments
	Key Resources		Channels	
Cost Structure			Revenue Streams	

Fig. 7.5: Template of the Business Model Canvas

DESIGN

The goal of this step is to generate and test viable business model options and select the best. Transform the results of data analysis from the previous phase into business model candidates. Strive for bold, new IoT business models. Question if your current business models and patterns can meet the challenges of the IoT world. Again, adopt the divergent thinking mode to brainstorm as many new model candidates as possible, and then switch to the convergent thinking mode to select the best one. Test the model candidates for you to make the decision. Testing can be done through experimenting different partnerships, revenue streams, distribution channels, and other components of the business model canvas.

After you have developed your new business model using the business model canvas, determine how it fits in the business model matrix that correlates the general business model patterns with the IoT business model patterns (Table 7.2), as discussed in chapter 4.

A study by PwC, a global network of consulting firms, has identified some growth opportunities for each of the IoT business model patterns. Study these opportunities carefully when developing your new business model candidates.[5]

		IoT BM Patterns					
		Modular hardware solutions	Virtual asset sharing	Data storage and brokerage	Data analytics and insights	Dynamic data bundling	Demater-ialized data feeds
General BM Patterns	Unbundling business models						
	The long tail						
	Multisided platforms						
	FREE as a business model						
	Open business models						

Table 7.2: Business Model Pattern Matrix

Opportunities for the Pattern of Modular Hardware Solution

Large companies offering modular hardware solutions can add more value to existing products, while smaller companies implement their solutions to every opportunity emerged from a wide range of market segments. These companies tend to stay in the B2B business and they see ample opportunities for acquisitions and corporate venturing. They typically generate revenue by licensing their solutions or their designs. Both large and small companies can find opportunities in the automotive industry, the energy sector, the healthcare industry, and the construction industry.

Opportunities for the Pattern of Pooled/Virtual Asset Sharing

Opportunities for virtual asset sharing companies come from variety of market segments, driven by the growing spread of "Uberization" across service sectors, and by the sharing economy gaining further maturity. These companies are typically in the B2C business, but more opportunities are emerging from the B2B market. Large companies are investing heavily in small, but rapidly growing tech companies and they also make acquisitions themselves.

Opportunities for the Pattern of Data Storage and Brokerage

Most of companies in this category do not have in-house capabilities for handling, storing, securing, and structuring the large and diverse data streams. The opportunities for them are on data storage and brokerage solutions and services since they position themselves between connected devices and sensors on one end, and applications that offer their customers insights, on the other.

Opportunities for the Pattern of Data Analytics and Insights

Opportunities for the companies in this category rise from three types of data analytics for advanced maintenance: descriptive, predictive, and prescriptive analysis. The outcome of descriptive analytics describes what has happened at a specific event through data aggregation and data mining. The results of predictive analytics predict what could happen during a future event through statistical modeling and forecasting. Prescriptive analytics answer the question of what agents should do to trigger a specific future event or to reach a desired state through automated optimization and simulation algorithms.

Opportunities for the Pattern of Dynamic Data Bundling

Opportunities emerge from a wide range of market segments for companies offering dynamic data bundling solutions. In the seafood production market, for example, data collected from sensors and cameras can be combined with satellite imaging data to improve the grow rate of shellfish. In the real estate market, bundled sensor data can be used to improve asset utilization. Opportunities in the healthcare market include mobile patient monitoring, hospital asset tracking, remote health check-ups, etc.

Opportunities for the Pattern of Dematerialized Data Feeds

There is an increasing demand for simplified user interface solutions that allow consumers and businesses to tap into real-time data streams relevant to their activities and interests, such as real-time road traffic data, performance of machinery and truck fleets, and health statistics of family members.

IMPLEMENT

After you have selected the best business model, implement its prototype in the field. Define all related projects and manage them using the project management tools. Pay attention to project milestones, legal structures, resources, budgets, risks, and results measurement. The process for managing IoT product development will be discussed in the next chapter.

MANAGE

The objective of this step is to adapt and modify the business model in response to market reaction. Continuously monitor the effect of changes in the market and in your organization on the effectiveness of your business model and modify the business model accordingly. This should become a companywide program that requires at least a dedicated person to manage your company's business model portfolio and to organize periodical workshops with cross-functional teams to evaluate and modify your business models.

CHAPTER EIGHT

HOW TO MANAGE IOT PRODUCT DEVELOPMENT

In chapter 6, you developed your vision statement and your business objective. To achieve your business objectives, you have developed your hierarchical business strategies across the entire organization, and you have designed your new business models (chapter 7). Now you need to develop IoT products to support your business strategies and your business models.

DESIGN FOR SIX SIGMA (DFSS)

Many companies follow the Design for Six Sigma (DFSS) methodology for new product development. DFSS is a customer-oriented design process that guides design teams to create something that is right the first time and accurately transfers the voice of the customer (VOC) into design solutions. The algorithm of DFSS is best described in the book Design for Six Sigma, A Roadmap for Product Development by Kai Yang and Basem El-Haik.[1] The roadmap has four phases, as depicted in Figure 8.0. IoT application of many tools used in the DFSS process will be discussed in chapter 10.

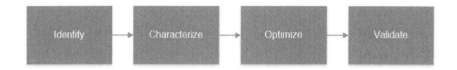

Fig. 8.0: Roadmap of Design for Six Sigma

IDENTIFY DESIGN OBJECTIVES

In this phase, a multifunctional project team is formed. The team investigates the VOC, transfers it into customer attributes (CAs), and map CAs with the functional requirements (FRs) of the design solutions.

Form a Multifunctional Team

The success of the development depends on the performance and collaboration of the team members from different business functions such as R&D, engineering, sales, marketing, and finance. The team must clearly define the roles and responsibilities of every team member at every phase of the process. The team leader is responsible for leading the team and continuously improving the team's performance.

Transfer the VOC into Customer Attributes

The team engages with customers to understand the VOC through various techniques described in chapter 3, then transfers the VOC into CAs—the analytical results of VOC data. Two tools are used for this purpose: the Kanol model and conjoint analysis. The Kano model helps the team identify the expected quality, normal quality, and exciting quality,[2] and conjoint analysis enables the team to determine how customers value the different attributes of a product and the trade-offs they are willing to make.[3] The Kano model and IoT application of conjoint analysis will be discussed in chapter 10.

Map CAs with FRs

Mapping CAs with FRs means determining a set of FRs of the design solutions and setting FR's specifications. FRs are the functional needs of the design solutions that satisfy the CAs. The action of mapping is accomplished using quality function deployment (QFD).

QFD identifies and classifies CAs along with their importance, correlates them with FRs, and then assigns specifications to the FRs.[4] As you can see later, QFD is also used in other two mappings in the DFSS roadmap.[5] IoT application of QFD will be discussed in chapter 10.

CHARACTERIZE DESIGN SOLUTIONS

Two mappings are performed in this phase. The first mapping is correlating FRs with design parameters (DPs)—the product design solutions that satisfy the FRs. The second mapping is correlating DPs with process variables (PVs)—the process elements that satisfy the specified DPs.

Map FRs with DPs

Producing a set of DPs to satisfy CAs is the central part of product design, involving determining a design concept and finalizing the functional structures of the product.

Determine Design Concept To come up with a right design concept is a challenging task. Two design tools are commonly applied to generate many design concept candidates and then select the best among them. These two tools are the theory of inventive problem solving (TRIZ) and the Pugh matrix.

Brainstorming is the most common method used for generating ideas. However, TRIZ is a more suitable tool for generating complex design concepts. TRIZ is a problem-solving mechanism derived from the evolution patterns of technological systems. TRIZ enhances the project team's ability to solve technical problems creatively because it is based on logic, data, and an algorithmic structure. The foundation of TRIZ is a set of laws that govern the evolution of technological systems. Upon this foundation, the algorithm inventive problem solving (ARIZ) is developed for conceptual designs.[6] TRIZ will be discussed in chapter 11.

The Pugh matrix is used to choose the best design concept among various alternatives by evaluating against a set of criteria and generating a hybrid which is better than any individual alternatives.[1] IoT application of Pugh matrix will be discussed in chapter 11.

Finalize the Functional Structure (Axiomatic Design) The selected concept must pass the "Axiomatic Test" to validate the independence of FRs and simplicity of the design concept.[7, 8]

Axiomatic design is a system design method that uses matrix methods to systematically analyze and improve the transformation of FRs into DPs. The two axioms in axiomatic design are the independence axiom (axiom one) and the information axiom (axiom two).

For a design to be conceptually robust, its concept must satisfy axioms one and two, as well as many corollaries. Axiom one requires a design concept to maintain the independence of the FRs, while axiom two requires a design concept to minimize its information content.

Per axiom one, if the FRs of a design concept have a 1:1 relationship with the DPs, a specific DP can be adjusted to satisfy its corresponding FR without affecting the other FRs.

Per axiom two, if the information content of a design concept is minimized, the design concept will have huge technological and cost advantages compared to a design concept with high information content. Design information content is a measure of the control system's complexity—the function of the number of variables and their inherent variations. Therefore, a design concept with minimum information content demonstrates organized simplicity, while a design concept with high information content represents disorganized complexity.

A design concept that satisfies axioms one and two overcomes the design's conceptual vulnerabilities. Several case studies, both IoTs and non-IoTs, of axiomatic design, will be discussed in chapter 12.

Map DPs with PVs

This is the last mapping in the DFSS algorithm which involves correlating DPs with a set of PVs. It is the central part of designing a manufacturing process for making the design product.1 Again, QFD is the basic tool used in this mapping.

OPTIMIZE DESIGN SOLUTION

Documenting design, assessing risks, and developing transfer functions are the major tasks in this phase.

Document Design and Assess Risks

Design scorecards are the tools for documenting design and assessing quality of the project progress.

Design scorecards collect, display, and analyze the facts of a product design or a process design in order to predict future performance of the product or the process and to indicate the need for improvement. The performance design scorecard is used for a product design and the process design scorecard is for a process design.[1]

Failure mode and effects analysis (FMEA) is used to evaluate the potential failure of a design and its effects, and to identify actions to prevent the potential failure from occurring.[9] Design FMEA (DFMEA) is used for a product design while process FMEA (PFMEA) is for a process design.[1]

Chapter 11 will give some examples of IoT applications of both design scorecards and FMEAs.

Develop Transfer Functions

While domain mapping gives us qualitative relationships between the critical design elements, the quantitative relationships are given by mathematical models—the transfer functions. Transfer functions that give quantitative relationships between FRs and DPs and between DPs and PVs are essential for product development. They help design teams understand how the typical values of the dependent variables change when any one of the independent variable changes.

In the transfer functions between FRs and DPs, FRs are dependent variables and DPs are independent variables. In the transfer functions between DPs and PVs, DPs become dependent variables and PVs are independent variables.

There are two common ways of developing transfer functions. The first way is to perform regression analysis on historical data. Regression analysis is a set of statistical processes for estimating the relationships between dependent variables and independent variables.

The second way of developing transfer functions is to perform regression analysis on data generated from a set of experiments that is systematically designed. This method is called design of experiment (DOE)—a generic statistical method that guides developing transfer functions. Taguchi robust parameter design is an advanced DOE—a systematic method that applies DOE to optimize designs by enhancing their transfer functions. It greatly improves the fundamental functions of engineering systems by maximizing the signal-to-noise (S/N) ratio, which compares the power of an engineering system's desired signal to the power of the background noise.[8, 10] Application of Taguchi robust parameter design on both IoT and non-IoT cases will be discussed in chapter 12.

VERIFY DESIGN SOLUTION

In this final phase, the design team verifies and validates design solutions and closes the project.

Pilot Runs

The team tests design solutions at the pilot facility and optimizes the design elements.

Validate Design

The team reviews the results of the pilot runs to ensure that product performance meets the product specifications (DPs). The team also ensures that PVs will be statistically stable in the manufacturing environment to produce high-quality products.

Launch Mass Production

At the final stage, the team hands over the entire design package to manufacturing and launches commercial rollout. It is important at this point to capture the lessons learned about the design process, to communicate the project termination, and to recognize the time and effort that went into the project.[5]

GATE REVIEWS

To ensure the quality of the development, each phase of the DFSS roadmap is followed by a gate review in which the management team reviews the results presented by the design team. There are three possible outcomes of the gate review:

1. The management team approves the completion of the current phase so the project will move to the next phase.

2. The management team is dissatisfied with the results and asks the design team to complete more work for the next review.

3. The management team decides to kill the project or put the project on hold.

PUT THEM ALL TOGETHER

I can imagine how hard it is for some readers to digest so much information of the DFSS roadmap packed into a single chapter. I hope Figure 8.1 will help you understand better the relationships between the tools discussed in this chapter.

IOT DFSS ROADMAP

The traditional DFSS roadmap, however, is somewhat rigid in implementation and relatively slow in responding to fast-changing markets. It is not uncommon to see a team that has strictly followed the DFSS process failures to develop an IoT product being accepted by customers simply because the market has changed during the period of product development.

To overcome this shortcoming, some IoT companies have embedded the plan-do-check-act (PDCA) cycles in each phase of the DFSS roadmap. The PDCA cycle was proposed by W. Edward Deming, the father of modern quality management. It is a four-step iterative management method for continuous improvement (Figure 8.2).[11]

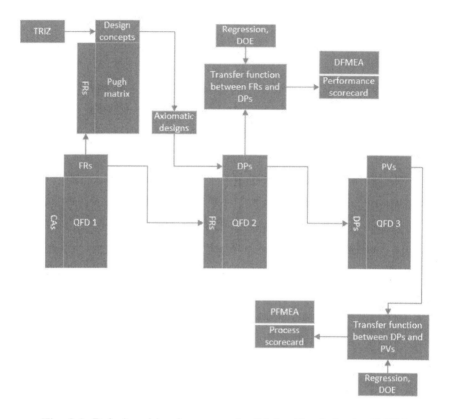

Fig. 8.1: Relationships between the Major Tools in the DFSS Roadmap

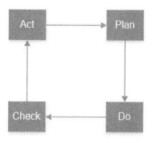

Fig. 8.2: Plan-Do-Check-Act Cycle

The first step is plan. At this step, the team assesses the current process and decides how to improve it.

The second step is do. At this step, the team enacts the plan, makes changes, and collects data.

The third step is check. At this step, the team analyzes the data to see what changes work best and checks if the results of the changes generate the expected outcomes.

The final phase is act. If the results of changes generate the expected outcomes, the team standardizes the changes. Otherwise, the team initiates a new PDCA cycle.

Embedding some PDCA cycles in each phase of the DFSS roadmap allows the team to plan in real time so the process is highly responsive and adaptive. At the end of each PDCA cycle, the team produces tangible results, either design concepts or prototypes, for customers to test, and then integrates customer feedback into next PDCA cycle to move the product closer to what customers want and need. The improved DFSS roadmap is demonstrated in Figure 8.3.

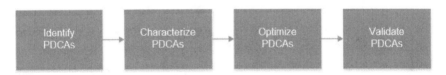

Fig. 8.3: Improved DFSS Roadmap

A process called Agile Stage-Gate process developed by Cooper and Sommer has a similar concept and structure as the one that we are discussing here. It has been implemented by a handful of leading IoT companies in North America and Europe, resulting in significant improvement in quality and speed of product development.[12]

CHAPTER NINE

HOW TO DEVELOP AN IOT ORGANIZATION

As the IoT transforms every corner of society, organizations must transform themselves in order to be successful in the IoT world. "In order to thrive in the Internet of Things landscape, organizations require greater talent with the skills to create algorithms and intelligence that will ultimately empower society to be that much better," says Caroline Tsay, the general manager of online business at Hewlett-Packard.[1] Developing an IoT organization is the responsibility of your senior leadership team as well as all the business departments in your organization.

SENIOR LEADERSHIP TEAM

Leadership is the key factor in transforming your company into an IoT organization. Your leadership team must focus on strategic planning and execution, nurture organizational IoT culture, and develop platforms for IoT monetization.

DEVELOP AND EXECUTE BUSINESS STRATEGIES

"IoT will impact the business models, corporate strategies, how some companies view and define their markets, and the investments that need to be made," said Maria Thomas, chief consumer officer of Smart Things, an open platform for home automation and IoT, which was acquired by Samsung in 2014.[2] To answer the challenges of the IoT's disruption and transformation, you have to set a clear vison about the future state of your company, as described in chapter 6. Share the vision with all the employees in your organization to get their buy-in so that every employee knows where your company is heading. However, having an inspiring vision itself is not good enough. To achieve the vision, develop your strategic objectives (chapter 6), your business strategies, and your new business models to win the IoT competition (chapter 7).

NUTURE AN IOT CULTURE

Taking a leap, removing silos, and analyzing data are key actions to ingrain an IoT culture.[2]

Take a leap

Be courageous, willing to take risks and pursue uncertain opportunities. You must be able to change the course quickly if your decisions have turned out to be wrong. In the IoT world, leadership is also "leaper-ship." "Many companies are waiting for IoT to be defined before they take action and invest," said Ulf Henriksson, president and CEO of Dematic, a global engineering and logistics company. "You have to define it yourself so you can tie a solution to it. If you cannot explain 'red,' how can you use 'red?' Dematic is implementing as it learns. One year down the line, we are still in search mode, but by beginning to define IoT, we're learning from it."[2]

Remove silos

The barriers between siloed departments in traditional organizations must be removed in order to synchronize the efforts of all departments. "You need a set of players," said Kenvin Ichhpurani, executive vice president and head of business development and strategic ecosystem at SAP. "There's not one person that's going to be able to do this all. You need to create virtual teams that have these different skill sets."[2]

Analyze data

Since the IoT will bring vast amounts of data to your company, your company needs expertise and skills on how to analyze data and how to convert data into value. While senior managers do not always need to be data scientists, they need to know how the IoT impacts your business and how to leverage data knowledge for new opportunities.

ESTABLISH MONITIZATION FRAMEWORKS

There are three rational frameworks you can use to boost assets, process, and product performance, and to identify new opportunities: enterprise financial performance, enterprise process economics, and performance improvement approaches.[3] Carefully analyze your company's current and future states and choose the framework that fits your company best.

Enterprise Financial Performance

This framework focuses on financial performance associated with revenue, expenses, and assets. Adopting this framework requires you to reduce the need for asset investment and to identify customer's needs that could be satisfied by new products and services.

Enterprise Process Economics

This framework focuses on the operating performance of the three core processes: customer life cycle, product life cycle, and facility life cycle. If you choose this framework, you must enhance these three life cycles.

Performance Improvement Approaches

This framework focuses on performance improvement. In this framework, you must systematically monitor and analyze processes to spot and address unexpected conditions and to harness the potential of new technologies used.

TECHNOLOGY DEPARTMENT

Deferent companies may have different names for their technology department such as research and development (R&D), engineering, information technology (IT), data science, customer support, etc. The technology department in this chapter refers to all the above business departments that are responsible for developing new products and services, including hardware and software, information technology, and data analytics.

ENABLE IOT PHILOSOPHY AND PRACTICE

The IoT will provide your company with many means to reduce costs and to improve efficiency. Communicate effectively with other departments and implement a data-based process improvement initiative throughout your organization. Educate all employees on the concept of big data, incorporate it into all business processes, and use big data's power to improve your company's relationship with your customers.[1]

ENACT AGILE DEVELOPMENT METHODOLOGY

Enact a development methodology to rapidly interact with customers, analyze customer data that are gushing in daily to ensure that your IoT products will meet and exceed customer expectations that are rapidly changing. The improved DFSS process described in chapter 8 is this kind of methodologies. This process consists of the stage-gate process based on the Design for Six Sigma algorithm with well-defined PDCA cycles embedded in each stage.

DEVELOP NEW PRODUCTS AND SERVICES

Explore innovation potential with the IoT technologies. The IoT products and processes you are developing must differentiate your company from your competitors. The ability to see the potential for innovation that your competitors do not will define your company's uniqueness in the marketplace. "The Internet of Things is forcing massive change on corporate IT," explains Sean Farney of Boston Consulting Group. "Those who identify, embrace, and empower their departmental domains to react to this emergent trend will thrive. Those who do not, will disappear."[1] Software and hardware development must become core competencies of your company, especially in mobile, back-end server, and cloud development.

ENHANCE DATA SECURITY

Be mindful of the vulnerability of your companies to security breaches. As the IoT is integrating with the public cloud, data confidentiality, integrity, and availability will be at increasing risk.[4]

In his book, *IoT Inc.*, Bruce Sinclair suggests a process for security best practices during the product development (Figure 9.0).[5]

Fig. 9.0: Security Best Practices in Product Development

Ideation

At the concept and ideation phase, clearly define security features and security requirements for your IoT products.

Design

Taking security requirements as the departmental requirements (FRs) of your design solutions, design a set of design parameters (DPs) and assess the relationships between the two sets of parameters using quality function deployment. Chapter 10 will discuss an IoT case study on quality function deployment. Integrating security functions into your product design early will avoid adding them in a later stage of product development or as a remedy after the security breach. Both are a recipe for disaster.

Development

During the development phase, try as much as you can to use the public security framework and the network segmentation by adding air gaps between networks. Encrypt key security parts of your products.

Testing

At this phase, scan security vulnerability of your IoT products and test their anti-penetration capability.

Release

During this phase, develop a procedure for reporting and fixing security vulnerabilities and develop a training program for training employees on identifying and fixing security vulnerabilities.[5]

SUPPORT AND MAINTENANCE DEPARTMENT

Your new business models may require you to serve your customer with the OTA (over-the-air) update mechanism. Your support and maintenance mechanism will gradually evolve from the reactive maintenance to eventually the prescriptive mechanism as shown in Figure 9.1.[6]

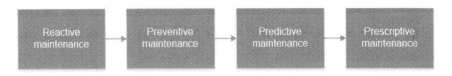

Fig. 9.1: Evolution of Maintenance Mechanism

REACTIVE MAINTEMANCE

This is the old method that many companies have used for decades. It is based on vendors' recommendations created by the vendors' technology department. The maintenance also includes on-time repair when something is broken. Reactive maintenance often is a part of time-based maintenance requirements in leasing or warranty terms. Reactive maintenance is an outdated and inefficient maintenance mechanism.

PREVENTIVE MAINTEMANCE

Instead of carrying out maintenance on a set schedule, preventive maintenance determines the need for maintenance of an asset based on its condition. This mechanism is only possible when sensors are embedded in the asset. The embedded sensors send real-time data to centralized systems that allow your technology department to diagnose the asset conditions and determine the need for maintenance before problems occur. Technologies such as edge computing are making it possible to determine the need for maintenance for moving or remote assets that can't be connected to Internet.

PREDICTIVE MAINTENANCE

Predictive maintenance is the next step of preventive maintenance mechanism which is rapidly adopted by some companies with advanced data-intensive processes. Those companies analyze the real-time data to evaluate the asset performance and reliability risks. Combining data from the asset with external data such as weather and geology, those companies can gain valuable insights beyond the traditional asset management system as part of a continuous improvement process.

PRESCRIPTIVE MAINTENANCE

Prescriptive maintenance goes one step further than predictive maintenance mechanisms by acting on the recommendations it has made based on the real-time data analytics. "Prescriptive maintenance requires that various asset management and maintenance systems are well integrated," said Matt Bellias, the head of worldwide marketing for Watson IoT's Asset & Facilities Management. "Systems like this must be 'cognitive,' or have the ability to think. This technology is at the intersection of big data, analytics, machine learning, and artificial intelligence. Companies such as IBM, with cognitive systems such as Watson and comprehensive enterprise asset management systems such as Maximo, are pioneering in this space."[6]

MARKETING AND SALES DEPARTMENT

Your marketing and sales department must analyze data from customers to understand their wants and needs, and it must personalize its marketing messages. Amy Cielinski, VP of marketing at Canara, a firm that provides infrastructure monitoring and predictive analytics, understands the importance of data reliability and analysis in successful marketing strategies. "We foresee increasingly detailed visibility as the Internet of Things continues to penetrate data centers and critical power infrastructure systems. We will need to expand, extend, and integrate to translate the data to information and predictive perspectives for our customers."[1]

Data from customers can be used to build models to prioritize product features and value propositions. Use the models in segmenting markets and in crafting personalized marketing messages based on specific application cases and sending those messages at the right time.[5]

Establish an IoT mindset that promotes IoT solutions based on valuation instead of on product features. Rather than trying to discover customers' pains, strive to deliver continuous IoT values to customers based on your business models. This practice will open up new opportunities of delivering more values to your customers.[5]

HUMAN RESOURCE (HR) DEPARTMENT

Your HR department must lead the efforts on nurturing an IoT culture, recruiting talents, training employees, and improving its own efficiency.

NURTURE AN IOT CULTURE

Your HR department must drive development of an IoT culture. Encourage your employees to take risks and to pursue uncertain opportunities in the IoT world. Promote cooperation and collaboration between business departments in data collection and analysis. Data-driven practice must be the corporate norm in making business decisions.

RECRUIT TALENTS

IoT business and technology requires a lot of new skills that your company may not have. Recruit actively new types of talent including chief information officers (CIOs), IoT architects, data scientists, IoT strategists and managers, software developers, security legal expert, IoT marketers, etc. Among them, high-quality CIOs, IoT architects, and data scientists are hard to find and retain.[7]

As the IoT demands grow and your company's IoT participation expands, you need a new type of CIO—a "CIO of everything," who can meet the challenges of expanded possibilities, increased complexity, and imperfect control.

The IoT architects must be able to design the IoT architecture and establish processes for IoT solution development.

Data scientists in IoT organizations must be able to use sophisticated analytic and simulation tools to transform a large amount of data into value. Some of the advanced IoT solutions require data scientists to develop digital twin models that pair the virtual and physical worlds to predict failures and opportunities.

TRAIN EMPLOYEES

Develop a program to train and educate all employees on IoT culture, philosophy, and technology. Not all employees need to be data scientists, but all of them must have the basic data analytic skills with a habit of making decisions based on data, not on experience alone.[5]

IMPROVE EFFECINCY

Once you have started your IoT journey, you will have a lot external and internal data. Use internal data to improve relationships and efficiencies. For example, you can analyze employee's health data and provide employees with health recommendations to minimize sick leave and reduce healthcare costs while ensuring the privacy of all employees.[1]

LEGAL DEPARTMENT

Your legal department will face unpredictable legal challenges in the IoT world since there is not much formal regulation on privacy and data collection. At the first step, set your own formal legal parameters and develop skills and procedures on data security, privacy, and contractual agreements with your customers, suppliers, and business partners. At the same time, watch the governmental and industrial legal and policy development, and comply with them accordingly.[1,5]

PART FOUR

TOOL BOX

We shall not fail or falter; we shall not weaken or tire. Neither the sudden shock of battle nor the long-drawn trials of vigilance and exertion will wear us down. Give us the tools and we will finish the job.

— Sir Winston Churchill

CHAPTER TEN

TOOLS FOR ANALYZING VOC DATA

In chapter 3, "What Is the Customer Asking For," we discussed the various methods of collecting data of the customer wants and needs—the voice of the customer (VOC). This chapter will discuss the tools used for analyzing VOC data, including the Kano model, affinity diagram, quality function deployment, and conjoint analysis.

KANO MODEL

The Kano model is developed for product development and customer satisfaction. It helps design teams understand customer preferences in product attributes to develop product specifications.[1]

THREE CATEGORIES OF PRODUCT ATTRIBUTES

The Kano model groups customer preferences on product attributes into three categories: expected quality, normal quality, and exciting quality, as shown in Table 10.0.

Product Attribute Category	Customer Satisfaction	
	With Attributes	Without Attributes
Expected quality	Neutral	Dissatisfaction
Normal quality	Satisfaction	Dissatisfaction
Exciting quality	Excitement	No dissatisfaction

Table 10.0: Three Categories of Product Attributes in the Kano Model

Expected Quality

The product attributes that belong to this group are the requirements that customers expect. If your products have those features, your customers take them for granted. Lacking any of those basic attributes will result in customers' dissatisfaction on your products.

Normal Quality

The product attributes in this group satisfy your customers. Without any of them, your customer will be dissatisfied.

Exciting Quality

The highest level of attributes is exciting quality. Your customers will be excited when they see those product attributes, but they will not be dissatisfied if those attributes are absent.

Attributes' places on the Kano model will change over time as shown in Figure 10.1. Even if your product attributes excite your customers today, they may drift to normal or even expected quality. Frequent analysis using the Kano model will offer you an insight on the competitive advantages of your product.[1]

Figure 10.0 demonstrates the relationships between product attributes and customer satisfaction.

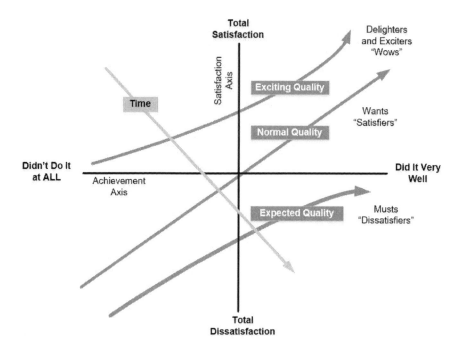

Fig. 10.0: Graphic Representation of the Kano Model HOW TO
USE THE KANO MODEL

Follow the procedure below to analyze VOC data using the Kano
model.

1. Collect VOC data from various means described in chapter 3.

2. Sort VOC data into three categories of the Kano model:
   expected, normal, and exciting quality.

3. Prioritize the customer needs using the multivoting or
   prioritization matrix. Both tools will be discussed in the next
   chapter.

4. Assign your current product attributes to the three categories of
   the Kano model.

5. Develop a plan to upgrade your product attributes from
   expected quality to normal quality, and from normal quality to
   exciting quality.

6. Frequently analyze new VOC data using the Kano model to gain insights of your product's competitive advantages over time.[2]

AFFINITY DIAGRAM

The affinity diagram is a method for grouping a large number of items into categories to make them easier to understand and handle. It is often used in brainstorming or in VOC data analysis to organize the items by their categories. The following procedure demonstrates how an affinity diagram is drawn to organize the VOC data:

1. Write customer wants and needs on Post-it Notes, one element per note.

2. Place the notes on butcher paper at random.

3. Sort the notes into groups.

4. Write a header card for every group that reflects the contents of the notes in the group.[2]

IOT MAILING

In chapter 2, we discussed an IoT application in mailing. Let's review the case.

Pitney Bowes, a provider of postage, mailing, shipping products and solutions, applies the IoT solution to create business value for its large-scale printing and mailing business. The company embedded hundreds of sensors on its inserters in the printing and mailing equipment that the company sells to its customers. The sensors send process data to local computers which are connected to the Internet through a Cisco 819 Integrated Service Router. Data are then transferred through the transport layer Security (TLS) connection and collected by GE's Predix platform. GE's analytics service performs data analysis through configuration, abstraction, and extensible modules. Through continuously monitoring inserters and issuing pre-failure alerts, the IoT solution has significantly improved service quality and reduce the service cost. Once an alarm appears that indicates a potential failure on an equipment at a customer site, service technicians will arrive there with the correct parts. With a large database that is continuously receiving data from customers, Pitney Bowes is developing benchmarks to help customers improve their productivity.[3]

AFFINITY DIAGRAM FOR IOT MAILING

Imagine you are the leader of the design team in Pitney Bowes. After many customer visits, your team has collected VOC data. Following the above procedure for the affinity diagram, you group the collected data into three categories:

1. We need to increase machine uptime.

2. We need to reduce the service cost.

3. We need to reduce operator errors.

Figure 10.1 is your complete affinity diagram. The notes on the first row are headers.

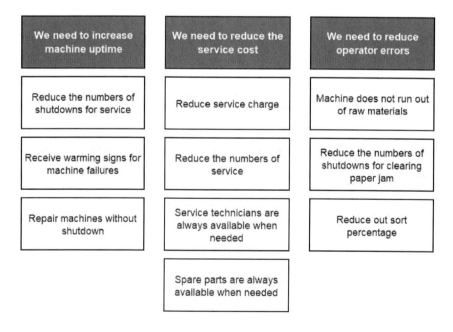

We need to increase machine uptime	We need to reduce the service cost	We need to reduce operator errors
Reduce the numbers of shutdowns for service	Reduce service charge	Machine does not run out of raw materials
Receive warming signs for machine failures	Reduce the numbers of service	Reduce the numbers of shutdowns for clearing paper jam
Repair machines without shutdown	Service technicians are always available when needed	Reduce out sort percentage
	Spare parts are always available when needed	

Fig. 10.1: Affinity Diagram for IoT Mailing

QUALITY FUNCTION DEPLOYMENT

Quality function deployment is a method to help design teams transform the VOC into functional requirements (FRs) of their design solutions.[4]

THE STRUCTURE OF QFD

The structure of QFD is like a house and therefore it is also called house of quality. It has seven areas as shown in Figure 10.2.[2]

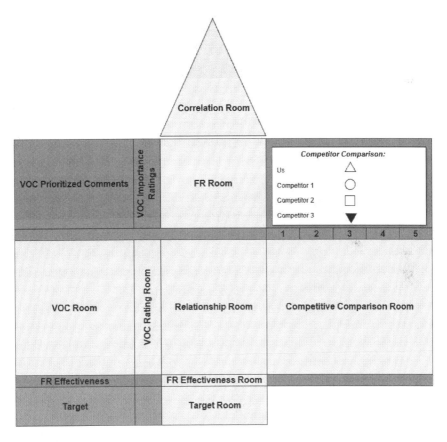

Fig. 10.2: Structure of Quality Function Deployment

The contents of each room are summarized in Table 10.1.

Room	Content
VOC	Prioritized customer needs
VOC Rating	Ratings on VOC importance from 1-5
FR	Functional requirements of design solutions
Relationship	Relationships between VOCs and FRs
Correlation	Correlation between FRs
FR Effectiveness	Effectiveness of FRs in satisfying customers
Target	Performance requirement for FRs
Competitive Comparison	Comparison of our product with competitors' products

Table 10.1: Contents of QFD Rooms

HOW TO CONSTRUCT A QFD

Follow the procedure below to construct your QFD:

1. List VOC items in the VOC room.

2. Rate importance of each of the VOC items in the VOC Rating room, using numbers 1 to 5, with value 1 being the least important and 5 being the most important.

3. Draw graphs in the Competitive Comparison room to show how customers perceive your products as compared to at least two competitors' products. Use a scale of 1 to 5 to rate performance with 5 being the perfect performance.

4. Determine the functional requirements (FR) of your products that may satisfy the customer needs.

5. List FRs in the FR room.

6. Assess relationship between each VOCs and each FR. Rate the relationship strength using value of 1 for low correlation, 3 for

medium correlation, and 9 for high correlation.

7. Record the relationship rating in the Relationship room.

8. Calculate effectiveness value of each FR in satisfying customers by first multiplying the relationship rating (1, 3, and 9) by the importance that VOC parameter and then summing up the products.

9. Record FR effectiveness values in the FR Effectiveness room.

10. Summarize the targets for FRs in the Target room.

11. Summarize the relationships between the FRs in the Correlation room, using the "+" symbol to indicate synergy and the "-" symbol to indicate conflicts.[2]

QFD FOR IOT MAILING

Let's go back to the IoT mailing case. As discussed before, you have summarized VOC data into three items using the affinity diagram. Now you want to design an IoT solution to satisfy three prioritized VOC items:

1. "We need to increase machine uptime," which has a highest importance rating: 5.

2. "We need to reduce the service cost." Its importance rating is also 5.

3. "We need to reduce operator errors." The importance rating of this VOC is 4, a little lower than the ratings of the previous two items.

After reviewing data collected on market, benchmarking, competitive analysis, and IoT technology development, the team generated a lot of FR candidates, and finally select three FRs which you believe will satisfy three VOC items:

1. Meantime to service: Meantime to service is a basic measure of the maintainability of repairable items. It represents the average

time required to repair a failed component or device. With increasing meantime to service, your customers can reduce the number of shutdowns for service, resulting in improved machine uptime.

2. Service accuracy: It is measured by the percentage of technicians arriving at the right time with the right parts.

3. Error trend analysis: It is provided to customers to help them reduce operator errors.

Following the procedure discussed above, you complete your QFD as shown in Figure 10.3.

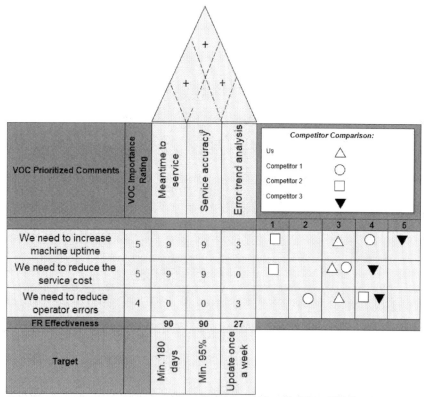

a: Service accuracy is measured by the percentage of technicians arriving at right time with right parts.

Fig. 10.3: QFD for IoT Mailing

CONJOINT ANALYSIS

Defining specification target values of the functional requirements is a very difficult task in constructing QFD. The traditional way of accomplishing this task involves utilizing historical targets and variation, competitive benchmarking, the Kano model, testing, and understanding competition trends. However, some questions often remain even after all the above means have been tried:

1. What is the customers' willingness to pay for the proposed product?

2. What are the trade-offs customers are willing to make among the various attributes that are under consideration in the new product design?

3. What is the accurate relative importance of each functional requirement?

4. What is the market share of a proposed new product among the current offerings of competitors?

Conjoint analysis is a powerful tool for answering above questions. It replaces the ineffective method of asking customers about each attribute in isolation with a model that allows us to infer the attributes' values based on the rating data from customers.[5]

CONJOINT ANALYSIS FOR IOT MAILING

In the IoT mailing case, you conduct a conjoint analysis through following steps. Design of Experiment (DOE) The conjoint analysis begins with a design of experiment (DOE)—a generic statistical method that guides developing transfer functions that link independent variables with dependent variables. In conjoint analysis, the independent variables are FRs and the dependent variable is customer ranking on FRs. In case of IoT mailing, you include two FRs in your study—meantime to service (MTTS) and service accuracy as measured by the percentage of technicians arriving at the right time with the right parts. You choose not to include error trend analysis because you believe the frequency of issuing reports once a week is enough to satisfy your customers. To study your customers' willingness to pay for several proposed products, you also include the price of the IoT solution in your study.

Your DOE now has three attributes (factors) and you have decided two levels for each of the attribute (Table 10.2).

Attribute	Level	Level Value
MTTS (day)	Low	90
	High	180
Service accuracy (%)	Low	90
	High	99
Price ($)	Low	5000
	High	10000

Table 10.2: Attribute Level Setting for Conjoint Analysis

A full factorial design consists of eight runs—eight potential products for each customer to rank. You replicate the DOE three times since they are going to visit four customers. The DOE table shown in Table 10.3.

Collecting Customer Ranking Data

You then visit four customers and ask each customer to rank the eight potential products from 1 to 8, with 1 being the most preferable product. You record the customer rankings in Column 8 in the DOE table (Table 10.4).

Regression Analysis

With the data collected, you perform regression analysis. The summary of analysis is shown in Table 10.5.

The regression model is:

Ranking = -12.000 + 0.03333 Mean time to service + 0.1667 Service quality – 0.0005 Price

C1	C2	C3	C4	C5	C6	C7
StdOrder	RunOrder	CenterPt	Blocks	MTTS	Service accuracy	Price
1	1	1	1	90	90	5000
2	2	1	1	180	90	5000
3	3	1	1	90	99	5000
4	4	1	1	180	99	5000
5	5	1	1	90	90	10000
6	6	1	1	180	90	10000
7	7	1	1	90	99	10000
8	8	1	1	180	99	10000
9	9	1	2	90	90	5000
10	10	1	2	180	90	5000
11	11	1	2	90	99	5000
12	12	1	2	180	99	5000
13	13	1	2	90	90	10000
14	14	1	2	180	90	10000
15	15	1	2	90	99	10000
16	16	1	2	180	99	10000
17	17	1	3	90	90	5000
18	18	1	3	180	90	5000
19	19	1	3	90	99	5000
20	20	1	3	180	99	5000
21	21	1	3	90	90	10000
22	22	1	3	180	90	10000
23	23	1	3	90	99	10000
24	24	1	3	180	99	10000
25	25	1	4	90	90	5000
26	26	1	4	180	90	5000
27	27	1	4	90	99	5000
28	28	1	4	180	99	5000
29	29	1	4	90	90	10000
30	30	1	4	180	90	10000
31	31	1	4	90	99	10000
32	32	1	4	180	99	10000

Table 10.3: Full Factorial DOE with 3 Replicates

C1	C2	C3	C4	C5	C6	C7	C8 ☑
StdOrder	RunOrder	CenterPt	Blocks	MTTS	Service accuracy	Price	Ranking
1	1	1	1	90	90	5000	5
2	2	1	1	180	90	5000	7
3	3	1	1	90	99	5000	6
4	4	1	1	180	99	5000	8
5	5	1	1	90	90	10000	1
6	6	1	1	180	90	10000	3
7	7	1	1	90	99	10000	2
8	8	1	1	180	99	10000	4
9	9	1	2	90	90	5000	2
10	10	1	2	180	90	5000	6
11	11	1	2	90	99	5000	4
12	12	1	2	180	99	5000	8
13	13	1	2	90	90	10000	1
14	14	1	2	180	90	10000	5
15	15	1	2	90	99	10000	3
16	16	1	2	180	99	10000	7
17	17	1	3	90	90	5000	5
18	18	1	3	180	90	5000	7
19	19	1	3	90	99	5000	6
20	20	1	3	180	99	5000	8
21	21	1	3	90	90	10000	1
22	22	1	3	180	90	10000	3
23	23	1	3	90	99	10000	2
24	24	1	3	180	99	10000	4
25	25	1	4	90	90	5000	2
26	26	1	4	180	90	5000	6
27	27	1	4	90	99	5000	4
28	28	1	4	180	99	5000	8
29	29	1	4	90	90	10000	1
30	30	1	4	180	90	10000	5
31	31	1	4	90	99	10000	3
32	32	1	4	180	99	10000	7

Table 10.4: DOE Table Containing Attributes and Customer Rankings

Model Summary

S	R-sq	R-sq(adj)	R-sq(pred)
1.05830	83.33%	79.33%	72.69%

Coded Coefficients

Term	Effect	Coef	SE Coef	T-Value	P-Value	VIF
Constant		4.500	0.187	24.05	0.000	
Blocks						
1		-0.000	0.324	-0.00	1.000	1.50
2		0.000	0.324	0.00	1.000	1.50
3		0.000	0.324	0.00	1.000	1.50
MTTS	3.000	1.500	0.187	8.02	0.000	1.00
Service accuracy	1.500	0.750	0.187	4.01	0.000	1.00
Price	-2.500	-1.250	0.187	-6.68	0.000	1.00

Regression Equation in Uncoded Units

Ranking = -12.00 + 0.03333 MTTS + 0.1667 Service accuracy - 0.000500 Price

Table 10.5: Regression Analysis of the DOE Data

R-sq(adj) is a statistical parameter that indicates the percentage of variations of dependent variables that can be explained by a given regression model. In this case, the value of R-sq(adj) is 79 percent, meaning 79 percent of variations of ranking value can be explained by the model.

The P value is another statistical parameter which, in this case, is used to judge if the effect of an attribute on customer ranking is significant. If the P value is less than 0.05, the effect is significant. Since the P values of all the attributes are zero, all of them have a significant effect on ranking, meaning all the three attributes are important to customers.

Utility Values

Using the coefficients of the attributes in the regression model developed, you calculate the utility value of every level of every attribute (Table 10.6). The utility values correspond to average customer preferences for the level of any given attribute. Within a given attribute, the utility values are scaled so the sum of them is zero. Therefore, the utility of every high level of a give attribute is the coefficient of that attribute, and that of the low level has the same absolute value, but with an opposite sign.

For example, the utility value of meantime to service (MTTS) at the high level, MTTS = 180, is the coefficient of MTTS, 0.0333, while that of the MTTS at the low level, MTTS = 90, is -0.0333.

Attribute	Level	Level Value	Utility
MTTS (day)	Low	90	-0.0333
	High	180	0.0333
Service accuracy (%)	Low	90	-0.1667
	High	99	0.1667
Price ($)	Low	5000	0.0005
	High	10000	-0.0005

Table 10.6: Utility Values of the Attribute Levels

Usually, customers' highest preference is always the best product with the lowest price. In this case, it is the service package with MTTS = 180 days, service accuracy = 99 percent, and price = $5,000.

Trade-Off Analysis

However, if this is too difficult for you to deliver, you need to know the trade-offs among the attributes. The overall utility of an ideal service package is:

Overall Utility = Utility (MTTS = 180) + Utility (Service Accuracy = 99) + Utility (Price = 5,000) = 0.0333 + 0.1667 + 0.0005 = 0.2005

From your market research, you know that customers currently purchase this kind of service at the price of $10,000. Therefore, the overall utility is:

Overall Utility = Utility (MTTS = 180) + Utility (Service Accuracy =

99) + Utility (Price = 10,000) = 0.0333 + 0.1667 + (-0.0005) = 0.1995

If you want to reduce price to $5,000, but keep service accuracy at 99 percent and customers' satisfaction unchanged, what should MTTS value be? This can be calculated by keeping overall utility at 0.1995.

Utility (MTTS) = 0.1995 (Overall Utility) − Utility (Service Accuracy = 99) − Utility (Price = 5,000) = 0.1995 − 0.1667 − 0.0005 = 0.0323

The MTTS Value per MTTS Utility is:

$$\frac{[180 \ (day) - 90 \ (day)]}{[\text{Utility (MTTS = 180)} - \text{Utility (MTTS = 90)}]}$$

$$= \frac{30 \ (day)}{[0.0333 - (-0.0333)]} = 450.4505 \ (Day/Utility)$$

The increased amount of MTTS Utility from Utility (MTTS = 90) to 0.0323 is:

0.0323 − (-0.0333) = 0.0656

Therefore, MTTS needed to keep customers as happy as today is:

90 (Day) + (Increased Amount of MTTS Utility) x (MTTS per Utility) = 90 (Day) + 0.0656 x 450.4505 (Day/Utility) = 120 (Day)

Compared to the service package your customers are purchasing today (MTTS = 180 days, service accuracy = 99 percent, and price = $10,000), the new service package (MTTS = 120 days, service accuracy = 99 percent, and price = $5,000) will not change your customers' satisfaction.

Market Share Estimation

You can also estimate the market share of a chosen product if you have the estimated utility values of your competitors' products, using the equation below.

$$Share_i = \frac{e^{U_i}}{\sum_{j=1}^{n} e^{U_j}}$$

where:

Ui is the estimated utility of your product i.

Uj is the estimated utility of a product in the market.

n is the total number of products in the competitive set, including your product i.

For example, if you want to calculate the estimated market share of your service package with an overall utility of 0.1995, and you know the overall utility values of three competitive products are 0.2112, 0.1750, and 0.1662.

The estimated market share of your service package is:

$$Share = \frac{e^{0.1995}}{(e^{0.1995} + e^{0.2112} + e^{0.1750} + e^{0.1662})}$$

The estimated market share of your product is 25 percent.

CHAPTER ELEVEN

TOOLS FOR IOT PRODUCT DEVELOPMENT, PART ONE

This chapter will discuss some common tools used in product development, including the Pugh matrix, failure mode and effects analysis (FMEA), design scorecards, and the theory of inventive problem solving (TRIZ). Two design crown jewels, axiomatic design and Taguchi robust parameter design, will be discussed separately in chapter 12.

PUGH MATRIX

The Pugh matrix is used to choose the best design concept among various alternatives by evaluating alternatives against a set of functional requirements for your design solutions (FRs), and to generate a hybrid design concept which is better than any individual alternatives.[1]

PROCEDURE FOR CONSTRUCTING THE PUGH MATRIX

The following procedure describes how to make and use the Pugh matrix:

1. Determine a baseline which is usually the median performance in the scope of the project.

2. Construct the matrix by putting a set of FRs in the first column, the name of the baseline in the head of the second column, and the names of the design concept alternatives in the head of each column that follows.

3. Compare each alternative with the baseline on every FR. Assign number 1 if the concept is better than the baseline, 0 if it is the same, and -1 if it is worse.

4. Sum up the ratings at the bottom of each column as shown in Table 11.0. The design concept with the highest rating is then chosen as the base for creating hybrid concepts. In Table 11.0, the chosen design concept is D because it has the highest rating.

FR	Baseline	A	B	C	D
1	0	1	-1	0	0
2	0	0	-1	1	1
3	0	1	1	-1	0
4	0	-1	0	0	1
SUM	0	1	-1	0	2

Table 11.0: Sample Pugh Matrix

5. Find the items in the chosen concept that have either a -1 or 0 rating and replace them with the items in other design concepts that have a highest rating. This will generate several hybrid concepts (Table 11.1).

FR	Baseline	A	B	C	D
1	0	1	-1	0	0
2	0	0	-1	1	1
3	0	1	1	-1	0
4	0	-1	0	0	1
SUM	0	1	-1	0	2

Table 11.1: Sample Pugh Matrix Hybrid Concepts

6. Select one hybrid concept as the new base line. In Table 12.1, the hybrid design concept indicated by the blue lines is chosen to be the new baseline.

7. Repeat Step 2 through 5 until you have a best hybrid concept (Table 11.2). In this case, the hybrid concept F (indicated by the orange lines in Table 11.1) is chosen as the final concept.

FR	Baseline (Blue)	F (Red)
1	0	0
2	0	0
3	0	1
4	0	0
SUM	0	1

Table 11.2: Sample Pugh Matrix for Choosing the Hybrid Design Concept

PUGH MATRIX FOR IOT MAILING

Recall the IoT for mailing case in chapter 10.2 After reviewing data collected on the VOC, benchmarking, competitive analysis, and STEEP analysis, you select three FRs among many FR candidates which you believe will satisfy three VOC items:

1. Meantime to service

2. Service accuracy as measured by the percentage of service technicians arriving at the right time with the right parts

3. Error trend analysis provided to customers

The QFD in Figure 11.0 shows the correlation between the VOCs and FRs.

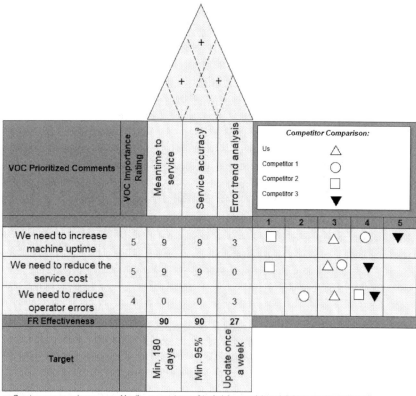

a: Service accuracy is measured by the percentage of technicians arriving at right time with right parts.

Fig. 11.0: QFD for IoT Mailing

Through brainstorming you generate two design concepts. To construct your Pugh matrix, you choose one of your competitors' IoT packages as the baseline. The IoT structures of the baseline and your design concepts are summarized in Table 11.3.

Following step one to four of the above procedure, you complete the Pugh matrix that compares your two design concepts with the baseline (Table 11.4).

Concept A is the best on service accuracy (measured by the percentage of service technicians arriving at the right time with the right parts) in the matrix due to its fastest speed in data transport, resulting in a quick response to impending failures. The fast speed is supported by the RTX equipped in Microsoft Window, the Cisco 819 4G integrated service router, and the TLS security protocol.

IoT Component	Baseline (Competitor)	A	B
Sensors	Hundreds of sensors are installed in servomotors to monitor the flow of mail and provide feedback to the control system	Hundreds of sensors are installed in servomotors to monitor the flow of mail and provide feedback to the control system	Hundreds of sensors are installed in servomotors to monitor the flow of mail and provide feedback to the control system
Local compute and storage	PC with ARM mounted inside machine and networked together to share data and synchronize control of the machine	PC with Intel Atom mounted inside machine and networked together to share data and synchronize control of the machine	PC with ARM mounted inside machine and networked together to share data and synchronize control of the machine
Computer software	Microsoft Windows	Microsoft Windows with a real-time extension (RTX)	Microsoft Windows with a real-time extension (RTX)
Integrated services router	Cisco 819 3G	Cisco 819 4G	Cisco 819 3G
Communication security	Security socket layer (SSL)	Transport layer security (TLS)	Security socket layer (SSL)
Application platform	Infrastructure as a service (IaaS)	Infrastructure as a service (IaaS)	Platform as a service (PaaS, GE's Predix)
Data analysis software	IBM SPSS	IBM SPSS	Predix's clarity advisor

Table 11.3: IoT Structures of the Baseline and the Design Concepts

FR	Baseline (Competitor)	A	B
Meantime to service	0	0	1
Service accuracy	0	1	0
Error analysis	0	0	1
SUM	0	1	2

Table 11.4: Pugh Matrix for IoT Mailing

Concept B is the best in the matrix in terms of meantime to service and error trend analysis, primarily due to GE's powerful PaaS platform Predix, and its statistical software Clarity Adviser.

Although concept B has a highest rating than the baseline and concept A, there is still a room for improvement. Since concept A is better than concept B on service accuracy due to concept B's faster speed generated by RIX, Cisco 819 4G, and TLS, adopting these components to replace those in concept B will generate a hybrid concept (Table 11.5).

IoT Component	Baseline (Competitor)	A	B
Sensors	Hundreds of sensors are installed in servomotors to monitor the flow of mail and provide feedback to the control system	Hundreds of sensors are installed in servomotors to monitor the flow of mail and provide feedback to the control system	Hundreds of sensors are installed in servomotors to monitor the flow of mail and provide feedback to the control system
Local compute and storage	PC with ARM mounted inside machine and networked together to share data and synchronize control of the machine	PC with Intel Atom mounted inside machine and networked together to share data and synchronize control of the machine	PC with ARM mounted inside machine and networked together to share data and synchronize control of the machine
Computer software	Microsoft Windows	Microsoft Windows with a real-time extension (RTX)	Microsoft Windows with a real-time extension (RTX)
Integrated services router	Cisco 819 3G	Cisco 819 4G	Cisco 819 3G
Communication security	Security socket layer (SSL)	Transport layer security (TLS)	Security socket layer (SSL)
Application platform	Infrastructure as a service (IaaS)	Infrastructure as a service (IaaS)	Platform as a service (PaaS, GE's Predix)
Data analysis software	IBM SPSS	IBM SPSS	Predix's clarity advisor

Table 11.5: IoT Mailing Hybrid Design Concept

Table 11.6 shows the IoT structures of your new baseline, concept B, and the hybrid concept C.

Comparing concept C with concept B using the Pugh matrix leads to the conclusion that concept C is better (Table 11.7). Therefore, you choose it as your design concept.

IoT Component	Baseline (B)	Hybrid (C)
Sensors	Hundreds of sensors are installed in servomotors to monitor the flow of mail and provide feedback to the control system	Hundreds of sensors are installed in servomotors to monitor the flow of mail and provide feedback to the control system
Local compute and storage	PC with ARM mounted inside machine and networked together to share data and synchronize control of the machine	PC with ARM mounted inside machine and networked together to share data and synchronize control of the machine
Computer software	Microsoft Windows with a real-time extension (RTX)	Microsoft Windows with a real-time extension (RTX)
Integrated services router	Cisco 819 3G	Cisco 819 4G
Communication security	Security socket layer (SSL)	Transport layer security (TLS)
Application platform	Platform as a service (PaaS, GE's Predix)	Platform as a service (PaaS, GE's Predix)
Data analysis software	Predix's clarity advisor	Predix's clarity advisor

Table 11.6: IoT Structures of Concept B and C

FR	Baseline (B)	C
Meantime to service	0	1
Service accuracy	0	0
Error analysis	0	1
SUM	0	2

Table 11.7: New IoT Mailing Pugh Matrix

DESIGN SCORECARDS

Design scorecards are the tools for documenting design and assessing quality of the design project progress.

Design scorecards collect, display, and analyze the facts of a product design or a process design in order to predict future performance of the product or process, and to indicate the need for improvement. The performance design scorecard is used for a product design while the process design scorecard is for a process design.[1]

DESIGN SCORECARD FOR AN IOT ACCELEROMETER

Accelerometer is an instrument for measuring acceleration of moving equipment or that involves the vibration of a machine.

Assume that your design team wants to develop a new accelerometer for an IoT application. This new accelerometer must have superior sensitivity and measurement range as compared to many products available in the market.

After you have designed this product, you make 2,000 accelerometers and you collect data used in the performance design scorecard to predict how well your new product will meet design parameter (DP) specifications.

Table 11.8 is your complete performance design scorecard.

Design Parameter	Unit	Target	LSL	USL	Mean	σ	Z LSL	Z USL	DPU	RTY
Sensitivity	mV/(m/s²)	20.0	19.0	21.0	19.9	0.60	1.5	1.8	1.00E-01	0.905
Measurement range	m/s²	0	-250	250	20	95.0	2.8	2.4	9.98E-03	0.990
Frequency range	Hz	8000	7200	8800	8000	190.0	4.2	4.2	2.57E-05	1.000
Non-linearity	%	0.5	na	1.0	0.4	0.15	na	4.0	4.00E-05	1.000
Transverse sensitivity	%	2.5	na	5.0	2.5	0.80	na	3.1	9.00E-04	0.999
Broadband resolution (1000Hz)	um/s²	2940	2881	2999	2930	16.0	3.1	4.3	1.11E-03	0.999
Setting time	s	1.0	na	2.0	1.0	0.26	na	3.8	6.00E-05	1.000
Discharge time constant	s	0.2	na	0.4	0.1	0.07	na	4.3	1.00E-05	1.000
								Total	1.12E-01	0.894

Table 11.8: Performance Design Scorecard for the IoT Accelerometer

PROCEDURE FOR DESIGN SCORECARD

1. Fill column 1 to 5 with names of DPs, their units, targets, lower specification limits (LSL), and upper specification limits (USL), respectively.

2. Collect your production data to calculate the mean (average) values of the DPs.

3. Calculate standard deviation (σ) values using the formula below. Where $\sum$ means "sum of," x is a value in the data set, $\overline{x}$ is the mean of the data set, and n is the number of data points in your data set.

$$\sigma = \sqrt{\frac{\sum |X - \overline{X}|^2}{n-1}}$$

4. Calculate Z score for LSL (Z LSL). Z score is the number of standard deviations between the mean and the specification limit. Z LSL is the number of standard deviations between the mean and LSL.

$$Z\ LSL = (Mean - LSL)\ /\sigma$$

5. Calculate Z scores for USL (Z USL). Z USL is the number of standard deviations between USL and the mean.

$$Z\ USL = (USL - Mean)\ /\sigma$$

6. Calculate defect per unit (DPU). DPU is the average number of defects per unit of your product. You can calculate DPU manually, using an Excel formula, or using a statistical software such as Minitab. Follow the steps below to calculate DPU using Minitab.

   a. Click on Cal tag, then select Probability Distribution, then Normal (Figure 11.1)

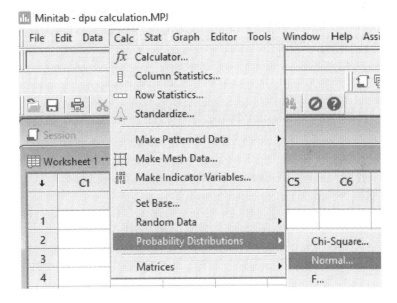

Fig. 11.1: Normal Probability Distribution Function in Minitab

   b. In the Normal Distribution window, type in the values of the mean and standard deviation. In the Input constant cell, type in the LSL value.

Figure 11.2 demonstrates how to do this for DP sensitivity.

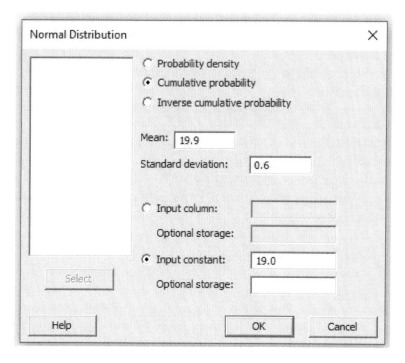

Fig. 11.2 Input Data in the Normal Distribution Window for Sensitivity

c. In Minitab's session window, you will find the value of the cumulative probability distribution outside LSL (Figure 12.3). The $P(X \leq x) = 0.0668072$ is the DPU LSL.

Cumulative Distribution Function

Normal with mean = 19.9 and standard deviation = 0.6

x	P(X ≤ x)
19	0.0668072

Fig. 11.3: Cumulative Probability Distribution Outside LSL

d. Repeat step a and b for DPU USL. In the Input constant cell of the Normal Distribution window (Fig. 11.2), type in the USL value instead.

e. In the cession window, you will find the cumulative probability distribution below USL, $P(X \leq x)$ (Figure 11.4).

DPU USL $= 1 - P(X \leq x) = 1 - 0.96623 = 0.0334$

Cumulative Distribution Function

Normal with mean = 19.9 and standard deviation = 0.6

x	$P(X \leq x)$
21	0.966623

Fig. 11.4: Cumulative Probability Distribution below USL

f. Calculate DPU for sensitivity.

Sensitivity DPU = DPU LSL + DPU USL = 0.0668 + 0.0334 = 0.1002

7. Calculate the rolled throughput yield (RTY).

$$RTY = e^{-DPU}$$

For sensitivity, $RTY = e^{-0.1002} = 0.905$

8. Calculate Total DPU. Total DPU is the sum of individual DPUs (DPU_i).

$$\text{Total DPU} = \Sigma DPU_i = 0.112$$

9. Calculate Total RTY. The total RTY is the product of individual RTYs.[3]

$$\text{Total RTY} = RTY1 \times RTY2 \times \ldots RTY_i = 0.894 = 89.4\%$$

The performance scorecard tells you the performance of your product by the values of its Z scores, DPUs and RTY. For DPs that has lower Z scores, especially those with Z scores less than 3, you need to improve your product performance.

FAILURE MODE AND EFFECTS ANALYSIS (FMEA)

FMEA is the tool used to identify all potential failure modes and their consequences, prioritize them based on a set of criteria, and take actions to eliminate or reduce the risks of the high priority failure modes.[4]

The following procedure depicts the way to construct FMEA:

1. List the entities such as steps of a process, components, or DPs of your product on the first column.

2. For each entity, list the possible failure modes.

3. For each failure mode, list its potential effects.

4. Rate the severity of each effect on a scale from 1 to 10, with 1 being most insignificant and 10 being catastrophic.

5. For each failure mode, list all the potential root causes.

6. Rate the occurrence of each cause on a scale from 1 to 10, with 1 being extremely unlikely and 10 inevitable. Occurrence is the probability of failure occurring for that root cause.

7. For each cause, list current process controls—the tests, procedures, or mechanisms in place to keep failures from effecting customers.

8. Rate detection of each control on a scale from 1 to 10, with 1 being absolutely capable of detecting the problem and 10 being incapable of detecting the problem.

9. Calculate the risk priority number (RPN). RPN is the base for risk prioritization.

   RPN = Severity x Occurrence x Detection

10. Recommend actions to reduce risks of the failure modes that have high RPN numbers.

11. Upon completion of recommended actions, recalculate RPNs to verify the effectiveness of the actions.

FMEA FOR IOT SMART AUTOMOTIVE BRAKING PRESSURE SYSTEM

Now assume you are the leader of a design team that is assigned to design a software for a brake by wire (BBW) system. The BBW system in automotive systems is the design concept where the mechanical or hydraulic system is replaced by electric/electronic systems. The electric/electronic systems are controlled by a computer embedded with a software.

Following the procedure above, you construct a FMEA (Table 11.9) to analyze the risks of your braking pressure control system.[5]

Design Parameter	Potential Failure Mode	Potential Failure Effect	SEV	Potential Cause	OCC	Current Control	DET	RPN	Actions Recommended
Braking pressure	Low pressure input	Late retardation may result in an accident	9	The dual braking system malfunctions	2	1. A dual braking system comprised of two tubes that exert pressure on brakes. When one system fails, the other one still works 2. A brake pressure switch will light up a signal on dashboard once the pressure in one of 2 tubes is lost 3. a smart sensor that can spot object in the line of motion and compensate required pressure to retard the vehicle appropriately	3	54	Install a smart sensor that can spot object in the line of motion and compensate required pressure to retard the vehicle appropriately
	High pressure input	Early retardation may lead to accident. For instance, a moving vehicle behind may brake late and run into the vehicle in its front	9	The dual braking system malfunctions	2	1. A dual braking system comprised of two tubes that exert pressure on brakes. When one system fails, the other one still works 2. A brake pressure switch will light up a signal on dashboard once the pressure in one of 2 tubes is lost 3. A rear smart sensor to detect the distance of the object behind	3	54	Install a rear smart sensor to detect the distance of the object behind
	No pressure	No braking may result in an severe accident	10	The input value fails	1	1. A dual braking system comprised of two tubes that exert pressure on brakes. When one system fails, the other one still works 2. A brake pressure switch will light up a signal on dashboard once the pressure in one of 2 tubes is lost 3. An emergency braking function that will be evoked when a null or zero value is detected	3	30	Provide emergency braking function that will be evoked when a null or zero value is detected

Table 11.9: FMEA for the BBW Pressure System

Since all the three potential failure modes may result in accidents, you want to add more detection and control to the control system to make your cars safer. Therefore, your team implements all the recommended actions. After all actions are completed, you run FMEA again to access the risk of your new system design (Table 11.10). The new added features reduce the detection rate from 3 to 1 for all potential failure modes, resulting in much lower RPN values.

Design Parameter	Potential Failure Mode	Potential Failure Effect	SEV	Potential Cause	OCC	Current Control	DET	RPN	Actions Recommended
Braking pressure	Low pressure input	Late retardation may result in an accident	9	The dual braking system malfunctions	2	1. A dual braking system comprised of two tubes that exert pressure on brakes. When one system fails, the other one still works 2. A brake pressure switch will light up a signal on dashboard once the pressure in one of 2 tubes is lost 3. a smart sensor that can spot object in the line of motion and compensate required pressure to retard the vehicle appropriately	1	18	
	High pressure input	Early retardation may lead to accident. For instance, a moving vehicle behind may brake late and run into the vehicle in its front	9	The dual braking system malfunctions	2	1. A dual braking system comprised of two tubes that exert pressure on brakes. When one system fails, the other one still works 2. A brake pressure switch will light up a signal on dashboard once the pressure in one of 2 tubes is lost 3. A rear smart sensor to detect the distance of the object behind	1	18	
	No pressure	No braking may result in an severe accident	10	The input value fails	1	1. A dual braking system comprised of two tubes that exert pressure on brakes. When one system fails, the other one still works 2. A brake pressure switch will light up a signal on dashboard once the pressure in one of 2 tubes is lost 3. An emergency braking function that will be evoked when a null or zero value is detected	1	10	

Table 11.10: FMEA for the Smart BBW Pressure System

THE THEORY OF INVENTIVE PROBLEM SOLVING (TRIZ)

The theory of inventive problem solving (TRIZ) is a problem-solving and product design methodology derived from the study of patterns of inventions in the global patent literature. In TRIZ, these patterns are summarized into certain laws—the laws of technological system evolution. Application of these laws leads to the recognition of the most likely next steps of evolution of a technological system, pointing a direction for developing next-generation technologies. Upon these laws a systematical method of problem solving is developed for conceptual system designs. This method is called the algorithm for inventive problem solving (ARIZ).[6]

LAWS OF TECHNOLOGICAL SYSTEM EVOLUTION

There are nine laws of technological system evolution in TRIZ:

1. Law of increasing degree of ideality

2. Law of nonuniform evolution of sub-systems

3. Law of increasing dynamism (flexibility)

4. Law of transition to a higher-level system

5. Law of transition to micro-level

6. Law of completeness

7. Law of shortening of energy flow path

8. Law of harmonization of rhythms

9. Law of increasing controllability

These laws describe the interactions between elements of a technological system, and between the system and the environment in which it evolves.[6]

Law of Increasing Degree of Ideality

The law of increasing degree of ideality maintains that technological systems evolve toward an increasing degree of ideality. The degree of ideality is measured by the benefit-to-cost ratio. Increasing degree of ideality means increasing capabilities of a product and decreasing its price, archived by reduction in size, weight, and cost while simultaneously adding capability.

Evolution of Apple iPod is an example of law of increasing ideality. The first generation of iPods was expensive and only functioned as a music playing device. Since then, the prices of iPod products keep dropping while their functionalities keep increasing, including those for playing movies and games, numerous applications, Wi-Fi connectivity, and e-mail capability.[7]

Law of Nonuniform Evolution of Sub-Systems

The law of nonuniform evolution of sub-systems states that the rates of evolution of various parts of a system are not the same. The nonuniform evolution creates conflicts, and it also offers opportunities for innovation by accelerating the slow evolution rates of the sub-systems.

An example of the law of nonuniform evolution of sub-systems is the development of wind farm technology. The fast evolution of turbine systems creates a conflict between power generation capability and capabilities of power transmission and storage. This conflict offers an opportunity for developing new power transmission and storage systems.[7]

Law of Increasing Dynamism (Flexibility)

Law of increasing dynamism (flexibility) maintains that technological systems evolve toward more flexible structures in order to adapt environmental changes. The need for adapting constantly changing environment demands increasing flexibility of technological systems.

Paper books have existed for centuries. They are heavy and expensive. The transcendence of the handheld technology and the Internet creates demands for new types of books that are light and inexpensive. That leads to the birth of electronic books that are rapidly replacing traditional paper books in the marketplace.[7]

Law of Transition to Higher-Level Systems

Law of transition to higher-level system states that technological systems evolve in a direction from a mono-system to a bi-system or a poly-system, that is, from a system performing only a single (mono) function to a system performing two (bi) or more (poly) functions.

The evolution of cell phones is an example of this law. Cell phones started with a mono-system, for phone conversations only. The military used the radio common carrier (RCC) that is a pre-cellular system. Motorola's DynaTac (brick phone) produced in the '80s marked the birth of cell phones. Motorola's MicroTAC in the late '80s is a bi-system comprised of the phone system and a calculator. The later bi-systems included Nokia's Candybar, the Elites, and the satellite phones. The launch of the personal digital assistants (PDA) in the '90s opened the floodgate of poly-systems. Palm's Palm Pilot launched in 1997 had multiple functions such as a virtual keyboard, handwriting recognition, and Internet connectivity. The poly-system products that follow suit are Motorola's Razr, Blackberry (including email function), T-Mobile's Sidekick (texting function), and Apple's iPhone that has all-in-one digital music player, camera, and an Internet-enabled PDA device, etc.

Law of Transition to Micro-Levels

The law of transition to micro-levels states that technological systems evolve from higher levels (macro-levels) to lower levels (micro-levels) of material structures, that is, from molecular aggregates to molecules, then to atoms and ions, and finally to elementary particles.

The development of weaponry follows this pattern: Traditional metal-based weapons operate at the molecular aggregate level. Chemical weapons are the best examples of those at the molecular level. They were outlawed by the Geneva protocol and the Chemical Weapon Convention. Nuclear weapons derive their destructive forces from nuclear reactions at the atomic level. Laser guns use lasers (elementary particles) to hit reflective targets. The most advanced one is the AN/SEQ-3 Laser Weapon System developed by the United States Navy.

Law of Completeness

The law of completeness maintains that an autonomous technological system consists of four principal parts: working means, transmission, engine, and control means. The engine is the primary energy source. The part of working means performs the primary function of the system. The transmission part transforms energy generated by the engine part, and the part of control means controls the parameter changes in the other three parts. Early technological systems usually required humans to perform the tasks of some principal parts. The evolution of technical systems frees humans from performing these tasks.

Autopilot cars free humans from driving cars directly. For example, Tesla cars' well-publicized feature is an advanced driver assistance system that uses cameras, sensors, and various vehicle systems to maintain speed, prevent the vehicle from running into slower-moving cars ahead, keep it in the lane, and even change lanes for drivers.

Law of Shortening of Energy Flow Path

The law of shortening of energy flow path maintains that technological systems evolve toward shortening the distance between the energy sources and working means. This can be achieved by reducing the number of energy transformations from one form to another or by reducing energy parameters such as mechanical reducers and electrical transformers.

The transformation of books from paper form to electronic form also serves as a good example of the law of shortening of energy flow path. Making paper books involves converting electric energy to mechanical energy, and shipping and storage involves many energy paths also. E-book production and distribution consumes very little energy with a very short energy path. Mail transformation from the paper mail to e-mails is another example of this law.

Law of Harmonization of Rhythms

The law of harmonization of rhythms states that an effective technological system always has good coordination of the periodicity of actions (or frequencies) of its parts. Ideally the movement of one part in the system should be fully synchronized with the movements of other parts of the system.

A fully automated vehicle is a system of micro-level harmonization of rhythms in which all the movements of individual components such as the steering wheel, the accelerator, the brake, and so on are synchronized by a computer. In the future, the entire system of all the automated vehicles on the road will be a system of macro-level harmonization of rhythms in which the movements of all vehicles on the road will be synchronized by a central computer system.

Law of Increasing Controllability

The law of increasing controllability maintains that technological systems evolve toward increasing controllability over the interactions among the system's components.

Smart home technology is the best example of the law of increasing controllability. In a smart home, any device that uses electricity can be put on the home network at owner's demand. These devices can be anything from lighting, home security, home theater and entertainment, appliances, and the thermostat. Whether the command be given by voice, remote control, tablet or smartphone, the home reacts.

ALGORITHM OF INVENTIVE PROBLEM SOLVING (ARIZ)

ARIZ combines all the TRIZ concepts and techniques in problem solving into one algorithm. These TRIZ concepts and techniques include ideal system, system conflict, physical contradiction, substance-field analysis, and the standards.[6]

Ideal System

An ideal system is a system whose function is fully performed without a physical entity. To move your system toward an ideal system, you need to concentrate on how to perform the function needed rather than how to improve the existing system performing the required function.

System Conflict

It is a common phenomenon that conflicts exist between different attributes of the system. Improving one attribute often results in deteriorating another attribute. It is TRIZ's goal to solve the system conflict by satisfying all conflicting requirements.

Physical Contradiction

Physical contradiction refers to a situation in which a component possesses two mutually exclusive physical states. The pattern of a physical contradiction can be described as "to perform action A1, the component (or its part) must have property P, but to perform (or to prevent, to neutralize) action A2, this component (or its part) must have an opposite property P." TRIZ offers some separation principles for solving the problems related to physical contradictions.

Substance-Field Analysis

The substance-field model describes the minimal technological system that performs only one function. A function performed by a tool or an object is accompanied by generation, absorption, or transformation of energy. The analysis of the interaction among the three components of the system—object, tool, and energy—is called substance-field analysis.

Standards

The standards in ARIZ are typical transformations of the minimal technological system from one substance field to another in order to improve the system. TRIZ provides a flowchart and an algorithm (ARIZ) for using them.

ARIZ

ARIZ consists of four phases as depicted in Figure 11.5.

1. Formation of system conflicts

2. Analysis of the system conflicts and formation of mini problems

3. Analysis of the available resources

4. Development of conceptual solutions

Details of ARIZ is out of the scope of this book. For more information on ARIZE, you can study the book *Innovation on Demand: New Product Development Using TRIZ* by Fey and Rivin.[6]

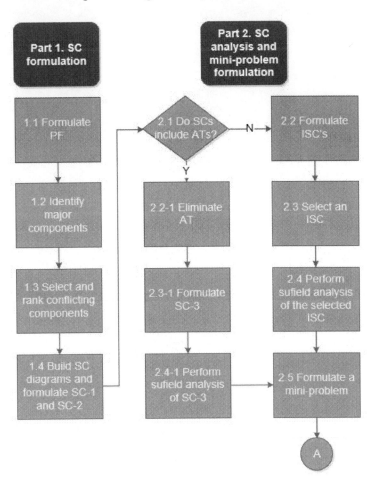

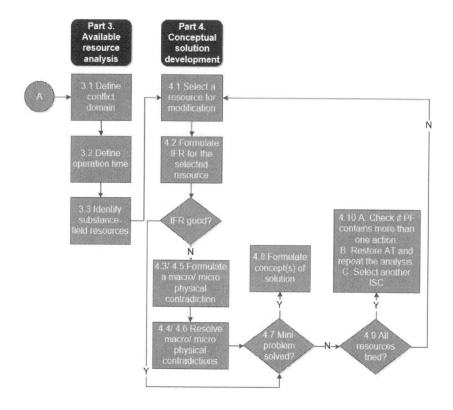

Fig. 11.5: Flow Chart of ARIZ

where:

SC: System conflicts

PF: Primary function

AT: Auxiliary tools

ISC: Intensified system conflicts

IFR: Ideal final results

CHAPTER TWELVE

TOOLS FOR IOT PRODUCT DEVELOPMENT, PART TWO

The improved DFSS roadmap discussed in chapter 8 is a customer-oriented design process that guides teams to create something that is right the first time and accurately transfers the voice of the customer into design solutions. To achieve this goal, design teams must overcome many vulnerabilities that lead to problematic quality issues.

These design vulnerabilities can be organized into two categories:

1. Conceptual vulnerabilities, which occur if a design lacks conceptual robustness.

2. Operational vulnerabilities, which lead to low operational robustness when the designed products are subjected to noise factors in the operational environment.

Fortunately, two design tools—axiomatic design and Taguchi robust parameter design—have been developed to overcome these vulnerabilities.

FOUR DOMAINS

There are four domains in the product development process, as shown in Figure 12.0:

1. Customer domain: The characteristics of the customer domain are customer attributes (CA), which are customers' expressions about their needs.

2. Functional domain: The key contents of this domain are functional requirements (FR), which are the functional needs of the design solutions that satisfy the CAs.

3. Physical domain: Design parameters (DP) are the central components of the physical domain. They are product design solutions that satisfy the FRs.

4. Process domain: This domain is represented by process variables (PV)—the process elements that satisfy the specified DPs.[1]

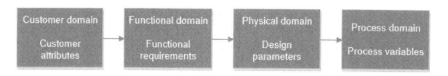

Figure 12.0: Four Domains in the Product Development Process

AXIOMATIC DESIGN

Axiomatic design is a system design method that uses matrix methods to systematically analyze and improve the transformation of FRs into DPs. An axiom is a premise that is taken to be true without proof—a starting point for further analysis and reasoning. The two axioms in axiomatic design are the independence axiom (axiom one) and the information axiom (axiom two).

For a design to be conceptually robust, its concept must satisfy axioms one and two, as well as many corollaries. Axiom one requires a design concept to maintain the independence of the FRs, while axiom two requires a design concept to minimize its information content.

Per axiom one, if the FRs of a design concept have a one-to-one relationship with the DPs, a specific DP can be adjusted to satisfy its corresponding FR without affecting the other FRs.

Per axiom two, if the information content of a design concept is minimized, the design concept will have huge technological and cost advantages compared to a design concept with high information content. Design information content is a measure of the control system's complexity—the function of the number of variables and their inherent variations. Therefore, a design concept with minimum information content demonstrates organized simplicity, while a design concept with high information content represents disorganized complexity.

AXIOMATIC DESIGN FOR A CONTROL SYSTEM

A customer asks the design team of an organization to design a control system for the customer's manufacturing process. The process has a storage tank for liquid chemical A and another tank for liquid chemical B. Each tank has a pump that moves the chemicals to a reactor, where chemical A reacts with chemical B to make a product (Figure 12.1).

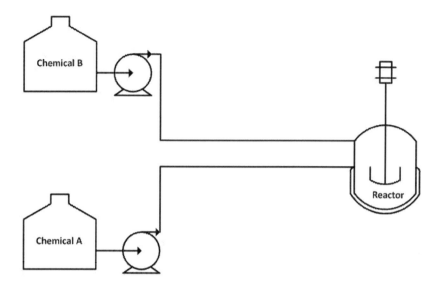

Figure 12.1: Manufacturing Process that Requires a Control System

The customer wants the control system to precisely control the total feeding speed of chemicals A and B, and to precisely control the chemical composition of the feeding stock. These needs are CAs.

After studying the CAs, the design team defines two FRs:

1. Control the total flow rate of chemicals A and B within 100 to 200 liters/minute (FR_1).

2. Control the ratio of chemical A to chemical B within 1.0 to 2.0 (FR_2).

The design team is confident that these two FRs will satisfy the two CAs. To satisfy the FRs, the design team develops the specifications (DPs) for the mechanical and electrical components of the control system, such as control valves, the inline flow meter, the composition analyzer and the electronic control loops. To satisfy the specific DPs, the team designs PVs for producing the mechanical and electronic components of the control system.[2]

A design concept that satisfies axioms one and two overcomes the design's conceptual vulnerabilities.[3]

Coupling Design

Continuing the example from earlier, the first design concept the design team proposes to the customer is to install a valve on each pipe that carries chemicals A and B to the reactor, as illustrated in Figure 12.2. In this design, the first DP is valve one turning and the second DP is valve two turning.

Based on the data from regression analysis and design of experiment (DOE), the design team develops transfer functions that correlate FRs and DPs:

$$\begin{bmatrix} FR_1 \\ FR_2 \end{bmatrix} = \begin{bmatrix} A_{11} & A_{12} \\ A_{21} & A_{22} \end{bmatrix} \begin{bmatrix} DP_1 \\ DP_2 \end{bmatrix}$$

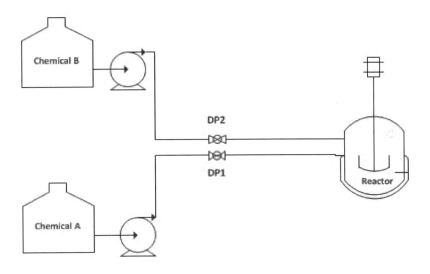

Figure 12.2: Coupling Design Concept

In a matrix, numbers are arranged in rows and columns. Multiplying two matrixes is possible only when the number of columns in the left matrix—the coefficient matrix in this example—is the same as the number of rows in the right matrix—the DP matrix. The equation above can be separated into two equations:

$$FR_1 = A_{11} \times DP_1 + A_{12} \times DP_2$$

$$FR_2 = A_{21} \times DP_1 + A_{22} \times DP_2$$

If the customer turns either valve one or valve two to change the total flow rate of A + B (FR_1), it inevitably changes the A/B ratio (FR_2), as well. Therefore, FRs in this design concept are not independent from each other—they are coupled with each other. This design lacks robustness at the conceptual level because it violates axiom one. The sign of a coupling design is a full or almost full coefficient matrix in its matrix transfer function equation.

Uncoupling Design

To uncouple the two FRs, the design team develops a new design concept in which there is a one-to-one relationship between FRs and DPs. In this concept, one valve is used to control the total flow rate of A+B, and a three-way valve is used to control the A/B ratio, as depicted in Figure 12.3.

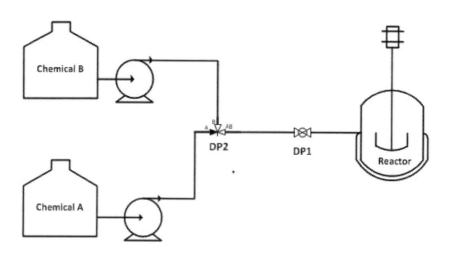

Figure 12.3: Uncoupling Design Concept

The following matrix transfer function equation correlates FRs and DPs:

$$\begin{bmatrix} FR_1 \\ FR_2 \end{bmatrix} = \begin{bmatrix} A_{11} & 0 \\ 0 & A_{22} \end{bmatrix} \begin{bmatrix} DP_1 \\ DP_2 \end{bmatrix}$$

This matrix equation can be separated into two equations:

$$FR_1 = A_{11} \times DP_1$$

$$FR_2 = A_{22} \times DP_2$$

In this design, the customer can turn valve one to adjust the flow rate of A + B (FR_1) without affecting the A/B ratio (FR_2), and it can turn valve two to change the A/B ratio without changing FR_1. Therefore, FRs in this concept are independent from each other. This design concept satisfies axiom one. This type of design is an uncoupling design in which FRs do not couple with each other. The sign of an uncoupling design is a diagonal line in its coefficient matrix in the matrix transfer function equation.

Sometimes, however, a total uncoupling design is too difficult or expensive to achieve. In that case, design teams should strive for a compromised solution called a decoupling design, such as:

$$\begin{bmatrix} FR_1 \\ FR_2 \end{bmatrix} = \begin{bmatrix} A_{11} & 0 \\ A_{21} & A_{22} \end{bmatrix} \begin{bmatrix} DP_1 \\ DP_2 \end{bmatrix}$$

A decoupling design has a triangle shape in its coefficient matrix of the matrix transfer function equation.

Simplified Uncoupling

Design After satisfying axiom one, axiom two must be satisfied—which means to minimize the information content of the uncoupling design. To do this, the design team develops a new concept that maintains FR independence with just one valve (Figure 12.4).

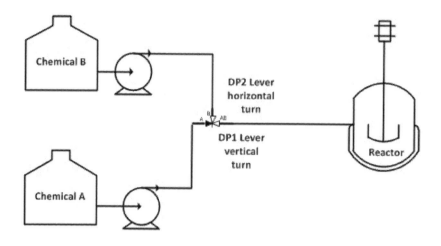

Figure 12.4: Simplified Uncoupling Design Concept

In this concept, the customer can turn the valve lever vertically to adjust the flow rate of A + B or horizontally to adjust the A/B ratio. Because this design reduces the number of valves from two to one, it reduces the number of variables in the control system. Therefore, not only does the design satisfy the independence axiom, it also satisfies axiom two by reducing the control system's complexity.[2]

AXIOMATIC DESIGN FOR IOT CNC MACHINE

Computer numerical control (CNC) is the automation of machine tools by a computer that executes preprogrammed sequences of machine control commands. In this design case, Axiomatic design is applied to the development of a system for monitoring and teleoperation of a CNC machine through the Internet.[4]

The design team develops the first level FRs based on the team's understanding of CAs.

FR_1: Monitor the manufacturing process remotely.

FR_2: Create interactivity between the process and the machine.

FR_3: Create an intuitive user interface.

FR$_4$: Define mechanisms for accessing historical data of the machine operation.

The team then maps the above FRs with the following DPs:

DP$_1$: Functions for web-based process monitoring

DP$_2$: Functions for machine configuration and control through the Internet

DP$_3$: Structured graphical user interface (GUI)

DP$_4$: System Query integrated with the machine operation database

Figure 12.5 IS the first-level transfer function.

Since the coefficient matrix in the transfer function equation is almost full, the design is significantly coupled. To uncouple the design, the design team decomposes the first-level FRs and DPs to form the second-level mapping. Table 12.0 lists the second-level FRs and their corresponding DPs.

$$
\begin{vmatrix} FR_1 \\ FR_2 \\ FR_3 \\ FR_4 \end{vmatrix} = \begin{vmatrix} A_{11} & A_{12} & A_{13} & A_{14} \\ A_{21} & A_{22} & A_{23} & A_{24} \\ & & A_{33} & \\ A_{41} & A_{42} & A_{43} & A_{44} \end{vmatrix} \begin{vmatrix} DP_1 \\ DP_2 \\ DP_3 \\ DP_4 \end{vmatrix}
$$

Fig. 12.5: First-Level Transfer Function

FR	Description	DP	Description
FR_1	Acquire power machine status (On/Off)	DP_1	OPC object to acquire
FR_2	Acquire the control mode	DP_2	OPC object to acquire the variable control mode
FR_3	Acquire machine door status	DP_3	OPC object to acquire the status of the machine door
FR_4	Acquire cooling status	DP_4	OPC object to acquire the status of the coolant system
FR_5	Acquire current feed-rate of the axes	DP_5	Method for getting actual feed rate
FR_6	Acquire axes' current position	DP_6	Method for getting axe position
FR_7	Acquire axes' load	DP_7	Method for getting axes' load
FR_8	Acquire alarms status	DP_8	Method for getting alarm description
FR_9	acquire the name of the running program	DP_9	Method for getting current program
FR_{10}	Acquire axes' rotation (spindle speed)	DP_{10}	Method for getting spindle speed
FR_{11}	Acquire travel distance for the spindles	DP_{11}	Method for getting distance to go
FR_{12}	Acquire configuration data	DP_{12}	Method for getting data setting
FR_{13}	Acquire images and audio from the shop-floor	DP_{13}	WebCam server

Table 12.0: Second-Level FRs and DPs

Figure 12.6 shows the second-level transfer function.

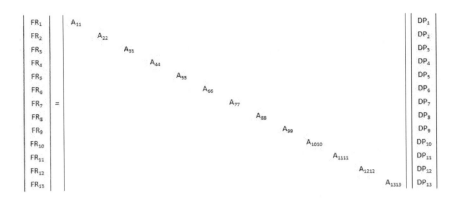

Figure 12.6: Second-Level Transfer Function

The diagonal line in its coefficient matrix in the transfer function equation indicates the design is uncoupled. Therefore, it satisfies the axiom one of axiomatic design.[4] It also satisfies the axiom two due to its simplified information.

TAGUCHI ROBUST PARAMETER DESIGN

Taguchi robust parameter design, another crown jewel of product design, is a systematic method that applies DOE to optimize designs by enhancing their transfer functions. It greatly improves the fundamental functions of engineering systems by maximizing the signal-to-noise (S/N) ratio, which compares the power of an engineering system's desired signal to the power of the background noise.[5]

THREE S/N CASES

For an engineering system to function effectively, the S/N ratio must be as large as possible. If the control system output must be at the target, it is the case of nominal-the-best. In this case, the S/N ratio is the logarithm of the ratio of average output to standard deviation:

$$S/N = 20 \log \left(\frac{\bar{y}}{s}\right)$$

Where S = the power of the control system signal, N = the power of the background noise, $\bar{y}$ = the average of the control system output, and s = the variation of the control system output.

If the control system output must be as small as possible, it is the case of the smaller-the-better. In this case, the S/N ratio is the negative log function of the average output square:

$$S/N = -10 \log\left(\frac{1}{n}\sum_{i=1}^{n} y_i^2\right)$$

Where n = the number of output y_i (i = 1, 2, ... n).

If the control system output must be as large as possible, it is the case of the larger-the-better. In this case, the S/N ratio is the negative log function of the average of the reversed output square:

$$S/N = -10 \log\left(\frac{1}{n}\sum_{i=1}^{n} \frac{1}{y_i^2}\right)$$

DESIGN OPTIMIZATION

For the smaller-the-better and the larger-the-better cases, the optimization strategy is simply to maximize the S/N ratio. For the nominal-the-best case, however, there are two steps involved in optimization, as illustrated in Figure 12.7.

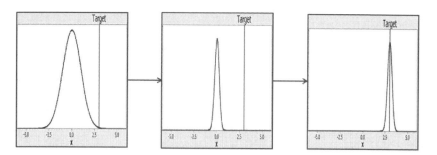

Figure 12.7: Two-Step Optimization Strategy

The first step is to find and adjust the significant DPs to maximize the S/N ratio. The significant DPs are those that have a significant effect on the S/N ratio.

The second step is to find and adjust the mean adjustment DPs to move the mean response to the target. The mean adjustment DPs are those that do not have a significant effect on the S/N ratio but have a significant effect on the mean.[5]

TAGUCHI ROBUST PARAMETER DESIGN FOR THE CONTROL SYSTEM

A special valve is the key component in the simplified uncoupling design concept in the case of designing a control system for the customer's manufacturing process described earlier. Therefore, the design team applies the two-step optimization strategy to optimize the design of the inner part of the valve. The prototype model, a hollow ball with holes on it, is shown in Figure 12.8.

Figure 12.8: Prototype Model of the Inner Part of the Special Valve

In this design, the control system output is the flow rate. The controllable factors are the ball wall thickness and the hole diameter of the prototype. The design team sets two levels for hole diameter at 100 millimeters and 110 millimeters, respectively, and two centimeters and three centimeters for ball wall thickness.

Environmental temperature is the uncontrollable factor. The design team sets the temperature at 10°C and 35°C in the DOE. Next, the team runs a DOE based on Taguchi L8 orthogonal array design and records the flow rate of chemicals A and B during each experiment in columns three and four of the DOE table (Table 12.1).

↓	C1	C2	C3	C4
	Diameter	Thickness	10C	35C
1	100	2	190.1	169.9
2	100	2	179.0	150.1
3	100	3	189.6	180.3
4	100	3	189.9	159.8
5	110	2	100.1	80.2
6	110	2	99.9	90.0
7	110	3	88.6	79.8
8	110	3	89.7	80.1

Table 12.1: DOE Table for the Special Valve Design

The design analyzer function in Minitab generates two main effects plots—one for S/N ratios (Figure 12.9) and one for means (Figure 12.10).

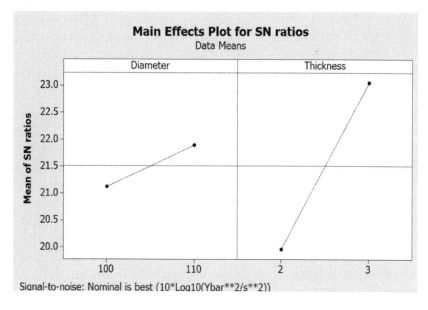

Figure 12.9: Main Effects Plot for S/N Ratios

The thickness of the ball wall is the important DP because it has a significant effect on the S/N ratio, as demonstrated by the steep main effect line in Figure 12.9. At the first optimization step, the design team sets the thickness at 3 centimeters to maximize the S/N ratio. The diameter is the mean adjustment DP because it doesn't have a significant effect on the S/N ratio, but it affects the mean significantly. At the second step, the design team sets the diameter at 103 millimeters to bring the mean flow rate to the target of 150 liters/minute.

By following the two-step optimization strategy, the design team successfully optimizes the operational functions of one of the major key components of the control system.[2]

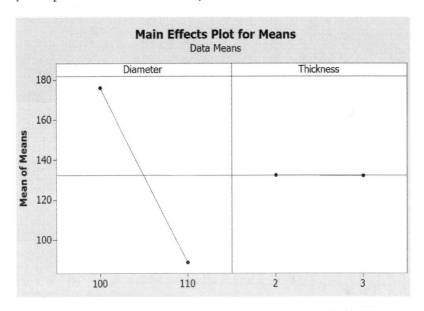

Figure 12.10: Main Effects Plot for Means

TAGUCHI ROBUST PARAMETER DESIGN FOR IOT IC WIRE BONDING PROCESS

Wire bonding process is the key process in an integrated circuit (IC) chip package. Designing the best process parameters is essential to meet the ever-increasing demand for process precision and fineness. One of the key parameters is the size of the ball that is on the end of the gold wire from the integrated circuit bond pad. The ball size and its variation must be minimized in order to achieve optimal wire bonding performance. In this design case, the design team, based on the historical data analysis, identifies five key process parameters in the wire bonding process: ultra-sonication (US) time, US power, bond force (BF), BF time, and search force (SF).[6] The team runs a DOE based on Taguchi L27 orthogonal array design that includes three levels for each of the five factors (Table 12.2). The team chooses three levels of vibration force, the noise factor, and records the ball sizes of the experimental runs under each of the noise factor level.

Factor	Unit	Level 1	Level 2	Level 3
US time	ms	5	8	10
US power	mW	120	160	200
BF	gf	10	15	18
BF time	ms	7	10	12
SF	gf	10	13	15

Table 12.2: Five Factors and Their 3-level Values in the DoE

The design analyzer function in Minitab generates two main effects plots—one for S/N ratios (Figure 12.11) and one for means (Figure 12.12).

Since this is the smaller-the-better case, the team optimizes the design by setting all factors at the level that maximize the S/N ratio: US time at 10 ms, US power at 120 mW, BF at 10 gf, BF time at 10 ms, and SF at 15 gf. The value of average ball size at this setting is 36.5 um, and S/N is -31.27, predicted by the transfer function.[6]

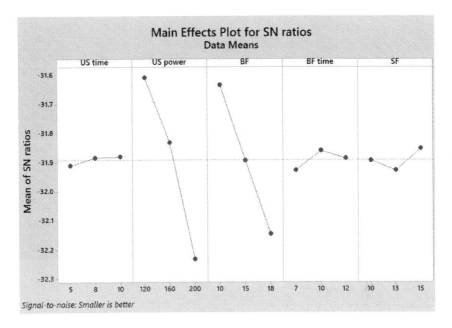

Figure 12.11: Main Effects Plot for S/N Ratios

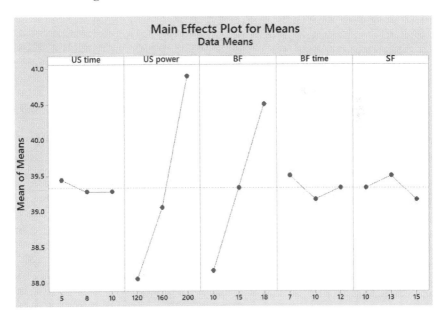

Figure 12.12: Main Effects Plot for Mean

NOTES

Chapter One: What Is the IoT?

1. Telecommunication Standardization Sector of International Telecommunication Union, ITU-T, Y.2060, "Overview of the Internet of Things," June 2012, https://www.itu.int/rec/T-REC-Y.2060-201206-I.

2. Timothy Chou, *Precision, Principles, Practices and Solutions for the Internet of Things,* Cloudbook, Inc., 2016.

3. Jacob Fraden, *Handbook of Morden Sensors: Physics, Design, and Applications, 5th ed.,* Springer, 2015.

4. Bruce Sinclair, *IoT Inc., How Your Company Can Use the Internet of Things to Win in the Outcome Economy,* McGraw Hill, 2017.

5. Felix Alvaro, *SQL: Easy SQL Programming & Database Management for Beginners,* Amazon Digital Services, 2016.

6. Ray J Rafaels, *Cloud Computing: From Beginning to End,* CreateSpace, 2015.

7. Viktor Mayer-Schonberger, Kenneth Cukier, *Big Data: A Revolution That Will Transform How We Live, Work, and Think,* Houghton Mifflin Harcourt, 2013.

8. Minitab, "Minitab 18 support," https://support.minitab.com/en-us/minitab/18/?SID=0.

9. Brian Everitt, Torsten Hothorn, *An Introduction to Applied Multivariate Analysis with R (Use R!),* Springer, 2011.

Chapter Two: Why the IoT?

1. Jonathan Vanian, *Ignore the Internet of Things at Your Own Risk,* November 3, 2015, http://fortune.com/2015/11/02/internet-of-things-irrelevant/.

2. Mobinius Admin, *Tech Roadmap for IoT – 2017,* February 21, 2017, https://www.mobinius.com/roadmap-for-iot-2017/.

3. Time, *Justin Trudeau, Jane Goodall and Others on Their Big Ideas for Changing the 2020s,* http://time.com/collection/davos-2019/5502586/big-ideas-2020s/.

4. Nicolas Windpassinger, *Digitize or Die, Transform Your Organization, Embrace the Digital Evolution, Rise Above the Competition,* IoT Hub, 2017.

5. Bruce Sinclair, *IoT Inc., How Your Company Can Use the Internet of Things to Win in the Outcome Economy,* McGraw Hill, 2017.

6. Timothy Chou, *Precision,* CrowdStory Publishing, 2016.

Chapter Three: What Is the Customer Asking for?

1. Michael Cowley, Ellen Domb, *Beyond Strategic Vision, Effective Corporate Action with Hoshin Planning,* Butterworth-Heinemann, 1997.
2. Edward F. McQuarrie, *Customer Visits, Building a Better Market Focus, Third Edition,* Routledge, 2015.

3. Dana Ginn, Evelyn Varner, Daniel Picard, Michele Kierstead, *The Design for Six Sigma memory Jogger, Tools and Methods for Robust Process and Products*, Goal/QPC, February 2004.

4. Claire Rowland, Elizabeth Goodman, Martin Charlier, Ann Light, Alfred Lui, *Design Connected Products, UX for the Consumer Internet of Things,* O'Reilly Media, 2015.

5. Donna Lanclos, "Post-Digital Learning Landscapes," April 17, 2014, http://www.donnalanclos.com/post-digital-learning-landscapes/.

Chapter Four: How Are You Doing?

1. Alexander Osterwalder, Yves Pigneur, *Business Model Generation,* John Wiley & Sons, 2010.

2. Ovidiu Vermesan et. al., European Platforms Initiative, "IoT Business Models Framework," http://www.internet-of-things-research.eu/pdf/D02_01_WP02_H2020_UNIFY-IoT_Final.pdf.

3. R.M. Dijkman, et. al, "Business Models for the Internet of Things," *International Journal of Information Management*, 35, 2015, pp. 672–678.

4. 4. PWC, "Cross-Cutting Business Models for IoT, A Study prepared for the European Commission," European Commision. 2017, https://clepa.eu/wp-content/uploads/2018/02/20180214-IoT.pdf.

5. Matthias Diez, Christian Ott, Silas Weber, "Business Models for the Internet of Things," December 22, 2016, http://docplayer.net/54167501-Business-models-for-the-internet-of-things.html.

6. Michael Cowley, Ellen Domb, *Beyond Strategic Vision, Effective Corporate Action with Hoshin Planning,* Routledge, 2012.

7. Timothy Chou, "Precision," CrowdStory Publishing, 2016.

8. Lucian Serna, *Tesla SWOT Analysis as a Great Business Model,* March 5, 2018, https://www.luckscout.com/tesla-swot-analysis/.

Chapter Five: What Is Your Business Environment?

1. Christopher E. Bogan, Michael J. English, *Benchmarking for Best Practices, Winning through Innovative Adaptation,* MdGraw Hill, 2014.

2. Bruce Sinclair, "IoT Inc., How Your Company Can Use the Internet of Things to Win in the Outcome Economy," McGraw Hill, 2017.

3. Michael Cowley, Ellen Domb, *Beyond Strategic Vision, Effective Corporate Action with Hoshin Planning,* Routledge, 2012.

4. J. DeLayne Stroud, "Understanding the Purpose and Use of Benchmarking," May 17, 2018, https://www.isixsigma.com/methodology/benchmarking/understanding-purpose-and-use-benchmarking/.

5. Alexander Osterwalder, Yves Pigneur, *Business Model Generation,* John Wiley & Sons, 2010.

6. PESTLEalaysis Contributor, "What is STEEP Analysis?" February 11, 2015, http://pestleanalysis.com/what-is-steep-analysis/.

Chapter Six: Where Do You Want to Be?

1. Michael Cowley, Ellen Domb, *Beyond Strategic Vision, Effective Corporate Action with Hoshin Planning,* Butterworth-Heinemann, 1997.

2. John Nemo, "What s NASA Janitot Can Teach us about Living a Bigger Life," December 23, 2014, https://www.bizjournals.com/bizjournals/how-to/growth-strategies/2014/12/what-a-nasa-janitor-can-teach-us.html.

3. "The Vision Statement and Mission Statement of Google," May 23, 2017, https://your-writers.net/blog/the-vision-statement-and-mission-statement-of-google.

4. Patrick, Hull, "Be Visionary. Think Big," December 19, 2012, https://www.forbes.com/sites/patrickhull/2012/12/19/be-visionary-think-big/.

5. Shu Liu, "Catching Fire, 7 Strategies to Ignite Your Team's Creativity," *Quality Progress,* pp. 18-24, May 2014.

6. Stephen R. Covey, *The Seven Habits of Highly Effective People, Powerful Lessons in Personal Change,* Simon & Schuster, Anniversary Edition, 2013.

7. Shu Liu, "Tool Time," *Quality Progress*, April 2013, pp. 30-36.

8. Christopher E. Bogan, Michael J. English, *Benchmarking for Best Practices, Winning through Innovative Adaptation,* MdGraw Hill, 2014.

Chapter Seven: How to Develop IoT Strategies

1. Michael Cowley, Ellen Domb, *Beyond Strategic Vision, Effective Corporate Action with Hoshin Planning,* Routledge, 2012.

2. Shu Liu, "Catching Fire, 7 Strategies to Ignite Your Team's Creativity," Quality Progress, May 2014, pp.18–24.

3. "The Vision Statement and Mission Statement of Google," May 23, 2017, https://your-writers.net/blog/the-vision-statement-and-mission-statement-of-google.

4. Alexander Osterwalder, Yves Pigneur, *Business Model Generation,* John Wiley & Sons, 2010.

5. PwC, "Cross-Cutting Business Models for IoT, A Study prepared for the European Commission," European Commision. 2017, https://iotevent.eu/wp-content/uploads/2015/05/BenchmarkStudyforLargeScalePilots intheareaofInternetofThings.pdf.

Chapter Eight: How to Manage IoT Product Development

1. Kai Yang, Basem S. El-Haik, *Design for Six Sigma, A Roadmap for Product Development, Second Edition*, McGraw Hill, 2003.

2. Jack B. Revelle, *Quality Essentials, A Reference Guide from A to Z*, ASQ Press, 2004.

3. Ronald T. Wilcox, *A Practical Guide to Conjoint Analysis, Kindle Edition*, Amazon Digital Service, 2003.

4. Joseph P. Ficalora, *Quality Function Deployment and Six Sigma, A QFP Handbook, Second Edition*, Prentice Hall, 2009.

5. Dana Ginn, Evelyn Vamer, *The Design for Six Sigma Memory Jogger: Tools and Methods for Robust Processes and Products*, Goal/QPC, 2011.

6. Victor Fey, Eugene Rivin, *Innovation on Demand: New Product Development Using TRIZ*, Cambridge University Press, 2005.

7. Basem El-Haik, *Axiomatic Quality, Integrating Axiomatic Design with Six-Sigma, Reliability, and Quality*, Wiley-Interscience, 2005.

8. Shu Liu, "The Crown Jewels of Design: Overcoming Vulnerabilities with Axiomatic and Taguchi Robust Parameter Designs," *Quality Progress*, February 2018, pp. 22-29.

9. D. H. Stamatis, *Failure Mode and Effect Analysis: FMEA from Theory to Execution*, ASQ Press, 2003.

10. Taguchi, Genichi, Subir Chowdhury and Yuin Wu, *Taguchi's Quality Engineering Handbook*, Wiley-Interscience, 2004.

11. APQC, *PDCA Instructional Cycle,* American Productivity & Quality Center, 2001.

12. Robert G. Cooper & Anita Friis Sommer, Agile–Stage-Gate for Manufacturers, Research-Technology Management, 61:2, 17-26, DOI: 10.1080/08956308.2018.1421380, 2018.

Chapter Nine: How to Develop an IoT organization

1. Stanton Chase, "The Internet of Things: Adapting Corporate Structure to Reflect the Connectivity of IoT," July 2015, https://www.stantonchase.com/wp-content/uploads/2015/07/IoT-White-Paper-Final-FR-1.pdf.

2. SpencerStuart, "Leadership for an Internet of Things World," January 5, 2016, https://www.spencerstuart.com/-/media/pdf%20files/research%20and%20insight%20pdfs/internetofthingsp2_010516.pdf.

3. John Hagel III, "Finding the Money in the Internet of Things," November 11, 2014, *Harvard Business Review,* https://hbr.org/2014/11/finding-the-money-in-the-internet-of-things

4. Wendy Zamora, "Internet of Things (IoT) Security: What is and What Should Never Be," December 22, 2017, https://blog.malwarebytes.com/101/2017/12/internet-things-iot-security-never/.

5. Bruce Sinclair, "IoT Inc., How Your Company Can Use the Internet of Things to Win in the Outcome Economy," McGraw Hill, 2017.

6. Matt Bellias, "The Evolution of Maintenance," March 14, 2017, https://www.ibm.com/blogs/internet-of-things/maintenance-evolution-prescriptive/.

7. Mark Hung, "Leading the IoT, Gartner Insights on How to Lead in a Connected World," April 2017, *Gartner,*

https://www.gartner.com/imagesrv/books/iot/iotEbook_digit
al.pdf.

Chapter Ten: Tools for Analyzing VOC Data

1. Jack B. Revelle, *Quality Essentials, A Reference Guide from A to Z,*
ASQ Press, 2004.

2. Dana Ginn, Evelyn Vamer, *The Design for Six Sigma Memory
Jogger: Tools and Methods for Robust Processes and Products,*
Goal/QPC, 2011.

3. Timothy Chou, "Precision," CrowdStory Publishing, 2016.

4. Joseph P. Ficalora, *Quality Function Deployment and Six Sigma, A
QFP Handbook, Second Edition,* Prentice Hall, 2009.

5. Ronald T. Wilcox, *A Practical Guide to Conjoint Analysis, Kindle
Edition,* Amazon Digital Service, 2003.

Chapter Eleven: Tools for IoT Product Development, Part One

1. Kai Yang, Basem S. El-Haik, *Design for Six Sigma, A Roadmap for
Product Development, Second Edition,* McGraw Hill, 2003.

2. Timothy Chou, "Precision," CrowdStory Publishing, 2016.

3. Dana Ginn, Evelyn Vamer, *The Design for Six Sigma Memory
Jogger: Tools and Methods for Robust Processes and Products,*
Goal/QPC, 2011.

4. D. H. Stamatis, *Failure Mode and Effect Analysis: FMEA from
Theory to Execution,* ASQ Press, 2003.

5. Shawulu Hunira Nggada, "Software Failure Analysis at
Architecture Level Using FMEA," *International Journal of Software
Engineering and Its Applications,* Vol. 6, No. 1, January 2012.

6. Victor Fey, Eugene Rivin, *Innovation on Demand: New Product Development Using TRIZ,* Cambridge University Press, 2005.

7. UKESSAYS, "The Laws of Technical systems Evolution Information Technology Essay," March 23, 2015, https://www.ukessays.com/essays/information-technology/the-laws-of-technical-systems-evolution-information-technology-essay.php?vref=1.

Chapter Twelve: Tools for IoT Product Development, Part Two

1. Kai Yang, Basem El-Haik. *Design for Six Sigma: A Roadmap for Product Development*, second edition, McGraw-Hill Professional, 2008.

2. Shu Liu. "Crown Jewels of Design: Overcoming Vulnerabilities with Axiomatic and Taguchi Robust parameter Designs," *Quality Progress*, February 2018, 22–28.

3. Basem El-Haik. *Axiomatic Quality: Integrating Axiomatic Design with Six-Sigma, Reliability, and Quality Engineering*, Wiley-Interscience, 2005.

4. Oliveria L.E.S., A. J. Alvares. "Axiomatic Design Applied to the Development of a system for Monitoring and Teleoperation of a CNC Machine through the Internet," Procedia CIRP 00 (2016)000-000, http://www.elsevier.com/locate/procedia.

5. Genichi Taguchi, Subir Chowdhury, Yuin Wu. *Taguchi's Quality Engineering Handbook*, Wiley-Interscience, 2004.

6. Jinn-Tsong Tsai, Cheng-Chung Chang, Wen-Ping Chen, Jyh-Horng Chou. "Optimal Parameter Design for IC Wire Bonding Process by Using Fuzzy Logic and Taguchi Method," 2169-3536 @ 2016 IEEE, http://www.ieee.org/publications_standards/publications/rights/index.html.

ABOUT THE AUTHOR

Dr. Shu Liu is a seasoned professional specialized in process optimization and machine learning. He has a PhD in chemistry from Virginia Polytechnic Institute and State University and an MBA from Robert Morris University. His various professional certifications (including data analyst and scientist, six sigma black belt and master black belt, lean master, quality manager, as well as TRIZ associate and practitioner) have enhanced his capabilities in managing R&D, engineering, and quality functions. Dr. Liu lives in Houston, Texas with his wife, Gusui Zhang.

Made in the USA
Columbia, SC
21 November 2019